FAMILY ADVENTURE GUIDE™

MASSACHUSETTS

"The Family Adventure Guide *series . . . enables parents to turn family travel into an exploration."*

—Alexandra Kennedy, Editor, *FamilyFun* magazine

D1513236

FAMILY ADVENTURE GUIDE™ SERIES

MASSACHUSETTS

FAMILY ADVENTURE GUIDE™

by

KELLY SPENCER

A VOYAGER BOOK

The Globe Pequot Press

OLD SAYBROOK, CONNECTICUT

Family Adventure Guide is a trademark of The Globe Pequot Press, Inc.

Cover Illustration by Lainé Roundy

All photos are by the author unless otherwise credited.

Library of Congress Cataloging-in-Publication Data

Spencer, Kelly.
    Massachusetts : family adventure guide / by Kelly Spencer. — 1st ed.
        p.   cm. — (Family adventure guide series)
    "A voyager book."
    Includes index.
    ISBN 1-56440-869-8
    1. Masschusetts—Guidebooks. 2. Family recreation—Massachusetts—
Guidebooks. I. Title. II. Series.
F62.3.S64   1997
917.4104'43—dc21   97–7091
                                                                      CIP

Manufactured in the United States of America
First Edition/Second Printing

To my parents, who infected me with the travel bug;
to Brian, travel and life companion extraordinaire;
and to Helen, who opens my eyes.

MASSACHUSETTS

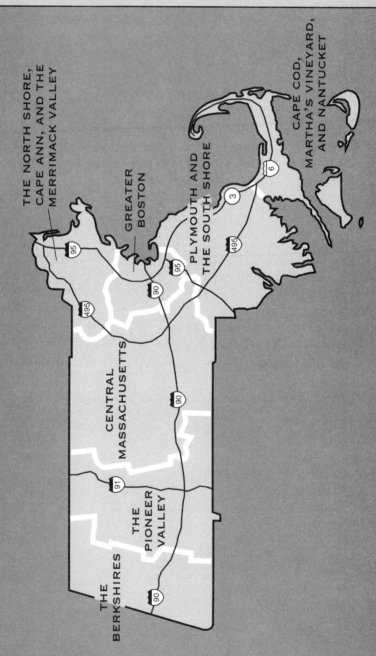

CONTENTS

The Pioneer Valley

- 111 -

The Berkshires

- 123 -

ACKNOWLEDGMENTS

The author thanks the Massachusetts Office of Travel and Tourism, the regional travel offices throughout the state, Joanne and Chuck Spencer, Janet, Bruce, and Sandra Wallace, Julia Crowley Carlson, and Kim Grant, who got me started on this gig.

INTRODUCTION

rowing up in an airline family that was almost always on the go means that I have had the fortune and opportunity to visit a lot of places in this country as well as in many others. Regardless of my age at the time, the places I've most enjoyed visiting have usually been those that weren't necessarily built with "family travel" in mind. I've never been mad about amusement parks, children's museums, or tourist traps that reek of commercial greed and leave much to be desired in terms of their historic or cultural significance, never mind how much fun you actually have while there.

Now that I am the mother of a daughter who is old enough to appreciate different environments, I've been able to put my well-hewn theories of family travel to the test. To my relief, I seem to be raising a born traveler. Our daughter enjoys visiting old houses as well as new restaurants, overgrown gardens and formal sculpture parks, large wildlife sanctuaries and small museums. At all these places she always has plenty of questions for us. We learn, too, from the startling observations that arise from her unjaded perspective.

While we're on the road, we avoid "family" restaurants with indoor play areas, toys scattered across the floor, and menus that are limited to hot dogs, grilled cheese sandwiches, and French fries. We don't need gimmicks in order to have a good time; we enjoy each other's company, and we love to spend many hours over the dinner table, wherever we are. When we have the choice, we much prefer staying in inns that welcome everyone from retirees to college students to families with toddlers. As you read this book, you'll see what I mean. With few exceptions, I've included only owner-managed restaurants, as well as lots of owner-managed inns, hotels, and motels. The rare exception to that rule is here because I checked it out and found it to be a place that my family would enjoy. If your family sounds like mine, you'll probably enjoy my—and our—selections. If you tend to enjoy the more kid-oriented types of eateries or motels, rest assured that you'll find them just about everywhere you go in Massachusetts, but I hope that you'll try something else, too. In this book I haven't counted out restaurants that serve alcohol, and I have included a few places that serve dinner only. I've also included a few gracious old inns that most people wouldn't think of as "family travel" types of accommodations. I suspect that there are other families out there like mine who don't limit themselves to McDonald's, Disneyland, and the Holiday Inn. They know that, given the opportunity, kids are supremely flexible and adaptable. Kids enjoy being trusted. They love to show that they can rise to the occasion.

I'm not a native of Massachusetts, but I've lived here longer than I've lived anywhere else. For me home has been, at various stages of my life, Germany, Scotland, Austria, Finland, northern California, and New York's Hudson Valley, as well as several apartments and houses in the Boston area. I settled in Boston after I finished college in California and realized that I missed the four-season life. Along with the extreme weather changes that come with the changes in the seasons, Massachusetts has a lot to offer its residents and visitors, and I've never tired of living here. It's been a great place to raise our young daughter. Some of New England's best beaches, prettiest orchards, lushest forests, and most challenging hiking areas are within a couple of hours' drive from our front door, not to mention the abundance of high-quality museums, galleries, and artists' studios that my daughter has been able to visit with her father, a curator, when she accompanies him on his frequent visits to artists and art organizations.

Researching a family-oriented travel guide is a family project, as well it should be. My daughter accompanied me, usually cheerfully, on return trips to favorite spots—the Cape, the Berkshires, the Vineyard, the Nashoba Valley—as well as on visits to less familiar areas of the state, including most notably the Quabbin Reservation and the Deerfield area.

We ate a lot of soup-and-sandwich lunches and drank a lot of milk (her) and ginger ale (me) during our searches for good restaurants that are appropriate for, though not limited to, families. After those long fact-finding days, we spent quiet nights in inns and motels, most of whose lodgings are included in this book, but some of which didn't make it: they were too loud, too dirty, too quaint, too disorganized, or falsely advertised as appropriate for families.

Writing a book about a place that you know well is tougher than you might expect. There's a lot more to it than simply making a list of your family's favorite places. When I began writing, I found that I had to backtrack because I didn't remember as much as I should about a lot of places I'd been before. Believe me, it was no chore to return to places like Wellfleet, Paul Revere's House, Bernardston, Old Sturbridge Village, Williamstown, Gay Head, and New Bedford. In fact, it was so much fun that I can't wait to do it all over again when it's time to write an update! Enjoy your own family research; you might want to make a game of creating your own supplemental Family Top Ten List for each region of Massachusetts. Keep your highway maps handy, look out for those Boston drivers, and, most of all, have fun.

FAMILY ADVENTURE GUIDE™

MASSACHUSETTS

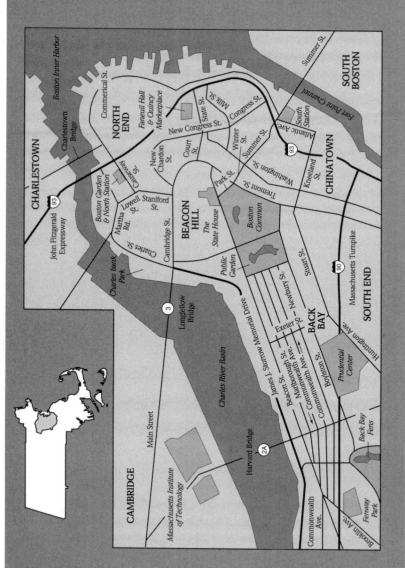

Greater Boston

Greater Boston

Chock-full of history, New England's largest city seems to have a significant site on every corner. Tourism has always been part of working life in busy Boston, and residents don't mind sharing their beautiful homes with visitors. They appreciate the smallness of the downtown area as much as you will. What's more, many of the older areas—the North End, Beacon Hill, and the Back Bay—are surprisingly compact and therefore eminently walkable for parents and kids alike.

Avoid restricting your journey to the sites along the well-trafficked red line of the Freedom Trail. Kids will enjoy the museums of Boston, especially the Museum of Science, the New England Aquarium, and the Children's and Computer Museums. Don't miss the bronze statues of Mrs. Mallard and her brood, the heroes of *Make Way for Ducklings,* near the pond in the Public Garden. And be sure to take a day or two to explore the nearby towns of Cambridge, Lexington, and Concord.

SOME PRACTICAL INFORMATION

Parking places are hard to come by in Boston. You'll enjoy your visit more if you leave the car in a parking garage and rely on your feet and public transportation to get around. The **Beantown Trolley** tours are another good resource (617–236–2148). The trolleys drive a ninety-minute loop to and through most of the sites your family will want to see. Get on and off the trolley as you wish throughout the day; it's better than a taxi.

Prices are $16.00 for adults, $5.00 for kids five to eleven, and free for kids under five.

Boston is an expensive place to stay. If you won't be staying with friends, plan well ahead to get the best prices. The hotels listed in this chapter offer family packages throughout the year, but you must reserve well ahead of time. An alternative is **Bed & Breakfast Agency of Boston** (47 Commercial Wharf, Boston; 800–248–9262), which maintains an extensive list of B&B accommodations around the city. They'll match your requirements and price range with an appropriate room, suite, efficiency, or apartment. Rates are $55–$130, double occupancy; kids under six stay free. Winter packages are great: three nights for the price of two.

BOSTON COMMON AND BEACON HILL

The best place to begin a Boston visit is at the corner of the **Boston Common** and Park Street. The **Boston Common Information Booth** (617–242–5642 for daily schedules of Freedom Trail tours) is a few yards from here. At the booth you can collect free maps, brochures, and information about sightseeing tours—and the central stop of the "T" (subway), Park Street, is right under your feet.

Boston Common is the beginning of the **Emerald Necklace,** the largest continuous green space through an urban center in the United States. The park system was designed by Frederick Law Olmsted in 1895 (among other acclaimed projects, Olmsted also designed New York's Central Park). From Boston Common the Necklace goes through the **Public Garden** to the **Commonwealth Avenue Mall,** the **Back Bay Fens,** through the **Muddy River** area, to **Olmsted Park, Jamaica Park,** and **Jamaica Pond,** and on to the **Arnold Arboretum** and **Arborway** before ending at the city's largest green space, **Franklin Park.** Sail, row, or fish at Jamaica Pond, bike and hike through any of the parks, play golf at Franklin Park, or hear concerts; there's usually something going on at one of the parks along the Necklace. For daily updates call the **Parks and Recreation Activities Eventline** (617–635–4006).

Just up the hill from the Park Street end of the Common is the impressive gold-domed **State House** (617–727–3676), built on John

Hancock's pasture in 1795. Along with the legislative chambers, the state capitol holds a collection of flags, costumes, and other remnants of the state's history. Frankly, though, from a family's point of view, the building is much more interesting from the outside than inside. Walk up the capitol's front steps and turn around to see a terrific view of the Common and the tops of the taller buildings of the Financial District; then, with the building behind you, look over to the right. You'll see a fine statue of the handsome young **John F. Kennedy,** whom the sculptor seems to have captured in midstride as he left Boston for the U.S. Senate, where he served before his presidency. Of the many JFK monuments scattered around Boston, Massachusetts, and New England, this is the most human. State House hours are Monday through Friday, 9:00 A.M.–5:00 P.M.; tours, Monday through Friday, 10:00 A.M.–4:00 P.M.

On a nice day Boston Common is worth a few hours' visit. Tell the kids to imagine what it was like when Boston residents used this "common" area to graze their cattle, then discuss what it may have been like to live here when British soldiers used the Common as a training ground before the Revolutionary War began (for an up-close view of domestic life during this period, be sure to visit Paul Revere's House in the North End). Walk through the Common to the Public Garden, which is separated from the Common by Charles Street.

A note of caution: Charles Street is a good place to alert everyone in the family to the fact that Boston's notoriously aggressive drivers earn their reputation on streets like this one. Parents should be extremely cautious—just because a stoplight has turned red doesn't mean that every car is going to stop, and there are plenty of Boston drivers who ignore stop signs, too. This flagrant disregard for the rules of the road is exacerbated by Boston's narrow, curving streets. Children must hold their parents' hands when they cross *any* street. Be careful, whether you're walking or driving.

Once you've crossed Charles Street and entered the Public Garden, walk to the right, toward Beacon Street. Here the kids will find the bronze sculptures of **Mrs. Mallard and her brood.** Ask the kids to name the ducks (*hint:* the first one is Jack . . .) and don't be surprised if you see childless adults snapping pictures of your kids playing on the ducklings; the sculptures look quite naked without kids on and around them.

The **African Meeting House** (8 Smith Court, at Joy Street on Beacon Hill; 617–742–5415) is the oldest standing African-American church in the country. Because of the racial tension of recent years, it may be hard to believe that Boston has a long history of abolitionism, but just after the Revolution, Massachusetts declared itself the first slave-free state, with full citizenry extended to black residents. Before and during the Civil War, this was the headquarters of the Underground Railroad, which helped many escaped slaves leave the South and find new homes and livelihoods in the North.

The **Black Heritage Trail,** operated by the National Park Service, is a tour of Beacon Hill–area buildings that are important to local and national black history. Along with the African Meeting House, stops include the **Hayden House,** an important stop along the Underground Railroad; the **Charles Street Meeting House,** where abolitionists Frederick Douglass and Sojourner Truth preached against slavery; and the **monument to Robert Gould Shaw and the Fifty-fourth Regiment,** which commemorates the first black division of the Union Army during the Civil War. Both the African Meeting House and the Black Heritage Trail operate year-round; admission, including the tour, is free.

The **Eliot & Pickett Houses** (6 Mt. Vernon Street; 617–248–8707) is a twenty-room B & B inn in two brick townhouses. Guests have use of the kitchens. Rates are $85 per night; children under eighteen stay free in their parents' room.

Beacon Hill Bed & Breakfast (27 Brimmer Street; 617–523–7376) is a brick rowhouse that overlooks the Charles River and has large bedrooms with fireplaces and private baths. Rates are $120–$145 per night.

The bar in the television program *Cheers* was modeled after the one that still exists in the **Bull & Finch** (84 Beacon Street; 617–227–9605). If your family must see this icon of contemporary America, you'll probably have to wait in a long line. Open daily, 11:00–1:30 A.M.

Louisburg Square (between Pinckney and Mt. Vernon streets), also on Beacon Hill, is a site of interest to *Little Women* fans: Louisa May Alcott and her family lived at number 10 after her success with *Little Women.* *Make Way for Ducklings* fans will remember the book's superb overhead view of the square. Long before Louisa's literary success, the Alcott family also lived at **20 Pinckney Street.** Nearby is the **House of Odd Windows** (24 Pinckney Street), whose facade boasts a wide variety of unusually shaped windows.

Walk back down to Charles Street, cross Beacon (carefully), and head for the lagoon in the Public Garden, where your family may well see real-life cousins of the Mallard family. In the spring or summer, the **Swan Boat ride** is a must. It's short—twelve minutes or so—and person-powered; a boatswain pedals the boat from his or her perch behind a wooden swan. Try to bring a bag of crumbs or peanuts along. The boats are on the lagoon from mid-April through mid-September, 10:00 A.M.–5:00 P.M. The fare is 75 cents for kids under thirteen and $1.25 for adults. Before or after your ride, be sure to check out the impressive statue of **George Washington astride his horse,** at the Commonwealth Avenue entrance to the Public Garden.

From the Public Garden walk back to the Common along the Tremont Street edge of the park. You may see a few softball games going on, and on summer weekends there may even be a free concert. At noon on any weekday, regardless of the weather, you're likely to share the park with many of the people who work in downtown businesses. They'll be walking through the Common, sitting on benches, and enjoying the fresh air and pleasant surroundings. There are quite a few good sandwich places within a few blocks of the Common. **Au Bon Pain** is always a safe bet for a made-to-order sandwich on freshly baked bread. There are several Au Bon Pain shops downtown; one is on Beacon Street near the corner of Park, and another is on Winter Street a block south of Tremont Street. **Souper Salad** is also a good choice, especially if you can't face one more sandwich; its salad bars are excellent, and its cookie selection isn't bad either. There's a Souper Salad on Summer Street, about 3 blocks south of Tremont Street, and another one on State Street, not far from Faneuil Hall.

DOWNTOWN

If your family is hungry for information about the city, or if you'd like to join a free ninety-minute guided tour of highlights of the Freedom Trail, walk over to the **National Historical Park Visitor Center,** right next to the Old State House (15 State Street; 617–242–5642). A plethora of free information is available at the center, from maps to books to helpful staff.

The small bookstore has an excellent collection of reasonably priced books about lesser-known people and events in Boston and New England history.

A good place for an informal sit-down lunch in the downtown area is **Fajitas & 'Ritas** (25 West Street; 617–426–1222), an innovative Tex-Mex-style eatery. Tables are covered with butcher paper, and patrons are encouraged to make use of the tubs of crayons. Delicious make-your-own fajitas as well as chili and tacos are served here. Open Monday through Wednesday, 1:00–9:00 P.M.; Thursday, 11:00 A.M.–10:00 P.M.; Friday, 11:00 A.M.–11:00 P.M.; and Saturday, noon–10:00 P.M.

The **Freedom Trail** is a 3-mile walking tour of sixteen of the city's colonial and Revolutionary landmarks. It's easy to find and to follow; just keep your eye out for the red line on the sidewalk. If your children are young, the walk as a whole may be too long; instead, you may wish to visit just a few of the landmarks. Be sure to pick up a map at the National Historical Park Visitor Center.

Covering part of the Freedom Trail as well as other sites that are of particular interest to kids, **Boston by Little Feet** (operated by Boston by Foot, 77 North Washington Street, Boston; 617–367–2345) is a family-oriented, one-hour tour of the downtown area that gives kids ages six through twelve a great introduction to Boston's history and architecture. Meet on Congress Street in front of the **Samuel Adams** statue. Tours are offered from May through October, Saturday at 10:00 A.M. and Sunday at 2:00 P.M. The fee is $5.00.

The **Omni Parker House** (60 School Street; 800–743–6664 or 617–227–8600) is a neat old hotel that's in a great location—everything is within a few minutes' walk from the front door, including the Common. Their minisuites are perfect for families and cost $129.

The brick **Old State House** (corner of Washington and State streets; 617–720–3291), built in 1713, is the oldest surviving public building in Boston. It manages to hold its own against the glass skyscrapers that surround it. Kids enjoy looking at the lion and unicorn on the building's gables. When the building was erected, it was the seat of the British government in the colonies, and these symbols of the Crown indicated that fact. The current lion and unicorn aren't the originals; when the Declaration of Independence was read from the building's rooftop in July 1776, Bostonians

KELLY'S TOP FAMILY ADVENTURES IN GREATER BOSTON

1. Museum of Science
2. Museum Wharf (Children's Museum, Computer Museum, Boston Tea Party Ship)
3. Duckling statues and Swan Boat ride at the Public Garden
4. New England Aquarium
5. Museum of Fine Arts
6. John Hancock Observatory
7. Isabella Stewart Gardner Museum
8. Drumlin Farm, South Lincoln
9. Old North Bridge, Concord
10. Orchard House, Concord

removed these symbols of the Crown and burned them. The lion and unicorn weren't replaced until quite recently. In the middle of the intersection in front of the building (Congress and State streets) is a star inside a ring of cobblestones, marking the **site of the Boston Massacre.** On March 5, 1770, a frightened group of British soldiers fired into a crowd of colonists who had gathered to protest recent crackdowns on customs duties and taxes. Though it was hardly a massacre, five people were killed on this spot, including a former slave, Crispus Attucks. Thereafter Sam Adams used the incident as a rallying point in his frequent speeches against the British.

Old South Meeting House (corner of Washington and Milk streets; 617–482–6439) began its life in 1729 as a church but quickly became a gathering place for political and revolutionary activity. The band of colonists who participated in the Boston Tea Party in 1773 dressed as "Indians" here before they sneaked down to the harbor. Today the meeting house serves as a museum to the colonial and Revolutionary period, with recordings of dramatized versions of public speeches during the period, a good gift shop, and an interesting model of Boston. Incidentally, Old South still has a political life: During campaign years politicians often use it as a venue for announcing their candidacies. Open daily, year-round, from April through October, 9:30 A.M.–5:00 P.M., and from November through March, 10:00 A.M.–4:00 P.M.

The **Granary Burying Ground** (next to the Park Street Church on Tremont Street, near the corner of Tremont and Park) is the final resting place of Paul Revere, John Hancock, Sam Adams, the five victims of the Boston Massacre, and the famous storyteller who was known as Mother Goose. No rubbings, please. Open year-round; free.

The **Boston Celtics** and **Boston Bruins** play at the brand-new **Fleet Center,** which replaced the venerable Boston Garden in 1995. For Celtics and Bruins tickets, call Ticketmaster (617–931–2000).

QUINCY MARKETPLACE AND THE NORTH END

Faneuil Hall is a historic site, a pedestrian zone, the entry to a massive shopping area, and a food market. Faneuil Hall itself was the site of many pre-Revolutionary meetings, which is why it's called "the cradle of liberty." Tell the kids to look for the tiny gold-plated grasshopper weathervane atop the building. Made in 1742, the grasshopper is a talisman. It's become one of Boston's symbols.

Beyond Faneuil Hall is copper-domed **Quincy Market,** in the center, and the **North** and **South Market** buildings on either side. The granite Greek Revival building has lived a long life as a marketplace—when it was built in 1826, the east portico was right on the edge of the harbor. The brick North and South Market buildings were built in subsequent years to accommodate the growing needs of the city's meat and produce whole-salers. In the 1970s the city hired an architectural firm to restore the build-ings and their surrounding cobblestone streets into an area that would be suitable for a pedestrian shopping area. Obviously, the project was a suc-cess; many tourists now come to Boston just to see the marketplace, and many locals, city employees, and people who work in the Financial District come here to eat lunch and people-watch.

The Quincy Market building itself is mostly devoted to take-out food vendors who sell everything from frozen yogurt to overstuffed deli sandwiches to pizza-by-the-slice to raw shellfish. Once your family members have gathered their lunch fixings, meet in the large center area, which is full of wide tables, chairs, and benches that are there for just this purpose. The North and South Market buildings hold shops and restaurants, from the kitschy to the upscale. Outdoors, regardless of the temperature, you're likely to see several street musicians, jugglers, mimes, and other performers. It's a fun place to spend an afternoon.

Walk along the east end of Quincy Market to **Haymarket,** an open-air market that's a sight in itself. Pick up the small kids and walk along the narrow aisles between stands of fruit, vegetables, and seafood. Prices are excellent, and you'd have a tough time finding a better example of where the locals go: This is where many North End chefs buy their produce.

Take the pedestrian passageway under the Fitzgerald Expressway; then hold the kids' hands (this is another of those notorious intersections) and wait until well after the light turns before you cross into the **North End,** an Italian neighborhood with excellent restaurants, terrific cafes, and fun festivals on most summer weekends, as well as several of Boston's most famous historic sites—which is appropriate since it's the oldest surviving neighborhood in the city.

Don't miss **Paul Revere's House** (19 North Square; 617–523–1676), the oldest house in Boston. Revere left from here to make his famous ride. It's a great place to ground your kids' idea of history; think about what it must have been like to live in such close quarters—and the Reveres weren't poor. Open daily from mid-April through October, 9:30 A.M.–5:15 P.M.; Tuesday through Sunday from November through mid-April, 9:30 A.M.–4:15 P.M. Admission is $2.00 for adults and 75 cents for kids five to seventeen.

Follow the Freedom Trail to Hanover Street and across the brick plaza called **Paul Revere Mall,** past the famous statue of Paul Revere, to the **Old North Church** (193 Salem Street; 617–523–6676). This is the site where, in 1775, Robert Newman, the church's sexton, hung two lanterns to alert Revere and his compatriots of the British troops' departure from Boston, by boat, on their way to Lexington and Concord to capture Sam Adams and

John Hancock. Open daily, 9:00 A.M.–5:00 P.M., except Thanksgiving and Christmas; Sunday services at 9:00 and 11:00 A.M. and 4:00 P.M.

One more historic site, this one a great spot for a picnic: **Copps Hill Burial Ground** has the city's best view of the waterfront—Charlestown, the Navy Yard, the USS *Constitution,* and Boston Harbor. There's a nice playground here, along with picnic tables and a shaded grassy area. Enter from Hull Street, between Snowhill and Charter streets. When you go in the Hull Street entrance, pause and look across the street at the **narrowest house in Boston** (9 feet 6 inches wide).

Most Boston families think of the North End as one big restaurant—there's something for everyone here, from thin-crust pizza to fresh seafood to family-style Italian restaurants with large tables and friendly wait staff.

At the original **Pizzeria Regina** (11½ Thatcher Street, 617–227–0765; no reservations) you'll find high-backed booths, no-nonsense service, pitchers of soft drinks, and delicious thin-crust pizza. You may encounter a line when you get here, since there are no reservations. It's worth the wait. Open Monday through Thursday, 11:00 A.M.–11:30 P.M.; Friday and Saturday, 11:00 A.M.–midnight; and Sunday, noon–11:00 P.M.

Pat's Pushcart (61 Endicott Street; 617–523–9616) is long on portions and short on decor (like many homes in the North End, it's wood-paneled and ceramic-tiled to excess). Upstairs is the better venue for families—tables are larger. The red sauce is fantastic. Note: Pat's closes for the month of July (when they're at their place in East Falmouth, on Cape Cod). Open for dinner only Tuesday through Saturday, 5:00–10:30 P.M.

If your family loves fresh seafood, don't miss the **Daily Catch** (323 Hanover Street; 617–523–8567; no reservations). Right on the busiest part of Hanover Street, this tiny restaurant is one of the best places to eat fish in seafood-loving Boston. The house specialty is calamari, but don't feel limited to squid dishes; everything's great. Although there's almost always a line waiting to sit at the six tables inside, the time will pass quickly because there are lots of nearby storefronts to peer into. Then there's the street life to watch. Ask the kids to listen for people speaking Italian. Open daily for lunch and dinner, 11:00 A.M.–10:30 P.M.

For a quick coffee, a slow gelato, or a leisurely look at true North End life, **Caffé Vittoria** (296 Hanover Street; 617–227–7606) is everyone's favorite choice. The decor is way over the top—faux marble tables, gilded mirrors, and garish murals of Italian seascapes—and that's all part of the dramatic scene. While the kids enjoy their gelato and the parents rejuvenate themselves with espresso or cappuccino, everyone should try to tune in to the scene here; it's as genuine an Italian cafe as you're likely to find in this country. Open daily, 8:00 A.M.–midnight.

Trio's (222 Hanover Street; 617–523–9636) is a fun place to watch the best pasta makers do their stuff. The Trio family makes an astonishing variety of pastas and sauces right here; ask if the kids can peek into the kitchen. If you have access to a kitchen yourselves, pick up the makings for a delicious dinner, or buy a ready-made lunch and find a bench. Open Monday through Saturday, 9:00 A.M.–6:00 P.M., and Sunday, 9:00 A.M.–1:00 P.M.

Mike's Pastry (300 Hanover Street, 617–742–3050) is another North End institution. The kids will marvel at the selection of pastries and cookies, and they'll probably enjoy watching the regulars coming in for the boxes of cookies they bring home or to the office. Open Monday, Wednesday, and Thursday, 8:00 A.M.–9:00 P.M.; Tuesday, 9:00 A.M.–6:00 P.M.; and Friday and Saturday, 8:00 A.M.–10:00 P.M.

Many North Enders say that Mike's is for the tourists, but **Bova's** (134 Salem Street; 617–523–5601) is the best Italian bakery in town. Who's to say, but this is a great place, with a more workaday environment than you'll see at Mike's, albeit with a more limited selection of goods. You're also more likely to be able to buy bread that's straight out of the oven here. Another reason why locals like it: It's open twenty-four hours a day.

WATERFRONT AREA

After all that food in the North End, the kids will probably need some room to run off their energy. Head to **Christopher Columbus/Waterfront Park;** it's one of the few places in Boston where people can actually relax on the waterfront without having to order something to eat. There's a nice playground (watch the little ones; the crow's nest is inviting, but the climb down is beyond most toddlers' abilities) and lots of room to stretch the legs. The rose garden is dedicated to **Rose Fitzgerald Kennedy,** the late matriarch of the Kennedy clan, who was born near here.

A note of caution: Along Boston's waterfront area there's no physical barrier to your child's tumbling into the water. Keep a sharp eye out.

For a short or long trip around the harbor or to nearby coastal towns, both **Boston Harbor Cruises** (1 Long Wharf; 617–227–4320) and **Massachusetts Bay Lines** (60 Rowes Wharf; 617–542–8000) offer inexpensive, regularly scheduled round-trips. Bring a lunch and a warm sweater or jacket; even on warm days the wind can be chilly out on the open water.

One of Boston's greatest attractions—for everyone, not only families —is the **New England Aquarium** (Central Wharf; 617–973–5200), and rightly so. Penguins, turtles, sea lions, and sharks share the stage with thousands of smaller fish, all contained by brilliantly designed tanks and pools. The four-story glass tank, wrapped by a spiral ramp, is the highlight of the aquarium—there's nothing like being eye to eye with a shark or walking up and down to follow a sea turtle's movements through the water. Plan to spend at least a couple of hours here, beginning with the harbor seal tank in front of the aquarium. Younger kids may be spooked, initially, by the dim lighting; show them that the only illumination in the aquarium comes from the tanks, and they'll probably forget their fear and become interested in the fish. Do use the opportunity to see the sea lion presentation (twenty minutes) aboard the *Discovery* pavilion that floats in the harbor beside the main building of the aquarium. Feeding time (five times a day) in the main tank is also worth waiting for: Scuba divers jump right in to feed the fish.

The aquarium operates a whale-watching tour from **Central Wharf** to **Stellwagen Bank,** the prime feeding grounds off the coast of Massachusetts; however, since this trip is long (about six hours, round-trip), it's much better to travel to Provincetown and make the much shorter boat trip from there (and enjoy the sights of Cape Cod, too). Open Monday, Tuesday, and Friday, 9:00 A.M.–6:00 P.M.; Wednesday and Thursday, 9:00 A.M.–8:00 P.M. (free admission after 4:00 P.M. Wednesday and Thursday); and weekends and holidays, 9:00 A.M.–6:00 P.M. Admission is $8.50 for adults and $4.50 for kids three to eleven.

When you manage to drag the kids out of the aquarium, walk along the harbor toward **Rowes Wharf** and the **Boston Harbor Hotel.** Walk through the wonderful six-story arch, then along the wharf area. You'll see lots of boats, large and small, pleasure and working.

Massport's **Water Shuttle** leaves and arrives from this wharf; it's a convenient way to get to and from the airport if you don't have a lot of luggage. *Note:* There are no bathrooms on board. For more information call their recorded info line: (800) 235–6426.

Continue along the wide wooden planks that border the city side of the harbor. When you reach the Northern Avenue Bridge, grab the kids' hands and cross it; then head for **Museum Wharf.** The wharf is home to two outstanding family attractions, the Computer Museum and the Children's Museum.

Best for families with school-age children, the **Computer Museum** (Museum Wharf; 617–426–2800) is the only museum of its kind in the world. The standout exhibit is the Walk-Through Computer™ 2000, a house-size version of a PC, complete with a keyboard and trackball that wouldn't be out of place on a playground. Other exhibits include Tools and Toys, which gives visitors a glimpse into the many worlds that are run by personal computers; People and Computers, a time-machine type of exhibit that places the early computers and the people who ran them in their historical contexts; and The Networked Planet, an explanation of how, when, and why the information superhighway touches our lives. The museum store is an excellent resource for families with computer-savvy kids; check out *The Computer Museum Guide to the Best Software for Kids* (HarperCollins Perennial). The museum is open daily during the summer, 10:00 A.M.–6:00 P.M., and Tuesday through Sunday during the winter, 10:00 A.M.–5:00 P.M. Admission is $7.00 for adults, $5.00 for kids over five, and free for kids under five. Fees are half-price 3:00–5:00 P.M. on Sunday.

Families shouldn't miss the **Children's Museum** (Museum Wharf; 617–426–8855). It's a hands-on romp of a place for every member of the family, with exhibits such as Teen Tokyo, about the lives of contemporary Japanese kids; the Kid's Bridge, which explores Boston's—and the country's—many cultures and ethnicities; Playspace, a toddlers-only play area;

Kids and museum staff play on a giant computer keyboard at the Computer Museum.
(Photo by John Rich/Courtesy FAYFOTO)

and the ever-popular two-story climbing structure, a vertical maze that stretches from the first floor to the second (don't let the little ones in here; you won't be able to fit yourself inside to get them out). Ask at the front desk about today's family-oriented activities; the museum serves as a clearinghouse for kids' activities around the city. Open daily, 9:00 A.M.–5:00 P.M. Admission is $8.00 for adults and $4.00 for kids six to fourteen.

After all the museum-going on Museum Wharf, you're likely to have worked up quite an appetite. During warm weather the **Milk Bottle** (Museum Wharf; 617–426–7074) has excellent salads, sandwiches, soup, and, of course, ice cream and frozen yogurt. The bottle was donated to the Children's Museum back in 1977 by the H. P. Hood Company, a large dairy. It would hold 50,000 gallons of milk. Open spring and summer, daily, 7:00 A.M.–9:00 P.M.

Nearby is **Bethany's** (332 Congress Street; 617–423–4042), a deli that provides lunches to the many creative service businesses in the area, not to mention the staffs of the Children's and Computer museums. There are a few tables inside, but the emphasis is on take-out.

During cooler weather **Lightships** (Museum Wharf; 617–350–6001) is the closest place to get a meal (other than fast food) when your family needs a food break at Museum Wharf. The view and environment are the thing here, rather than the food (which isn't bad, just not spectacular); windows everywhere on this floating restaurant bring in the view of the city skyline and the busy harbor that surrounds Museum Wharf. Open daily year-round, 11:30–1:30 A.M.

When you're ready to leave Museum Wharf, head for the Congress Street Bridge (with your back to the museum building, it's the one on the left, just behind Lightships). You'll walk right past the **Boston Tea Party Ship and Museum** (off the Congress Street Bridge; 617–338–1773). Of course, it's not the real ship, but it's a good facsimile of the *Beaver,* and the "colonists" on board can help the kids retell the story that everyone knows: In 1773, to protest the high taxes imposed by the Crown on tea, ninety Boston revolutionaries dressed in "Indian" regalia at Old South Meeting House and, accompanied by a large group of sympathizers, made their way to the *Beaver* and threw the ship's contents—340 chests full of tea—into the harbor. Rather than paying for everyone to go on the ship, you may want to satisfy your curiosity by looking at it from the bridge. If you do go on board, however, the kids will be able to toss "tea chests" overboard themselves. From March through Memorial Day and from Labor Day through November, open daily 9:00 A.M.–5:00 P.M.; from Memorial Day to Labor Day, open daily 9:00 A.M.–6:00 P.M.; closed December, January, and February. Admission is $6.00 for adults and $3.00 for kids five to fifteen.

Just a couple of blocks from the Congress Street Bridge, recently restored and renovated **South Station** has a pleasant food court area and lots of tables. It's a good place to have lunch and let the kids stretch their legs a bit; since it's not a restaurant, no one minds if they run around.

CHINATOWN AND DOWNTOWN CROSSING

From South Station it's a short walk to Chinatown. As in most Chinatowns around the world, this part of town bursts with tiny, inexpensive restaurants. One of the best is **Chau Chow** (52 Beach Street; 617–426–6266), which specializes in seafood, but everything's good. Open daily from 10:00–2:00 A.M.

An unexpected treat in Chinatown is **Jacob Wirth** (37 Stuart Street; 617–338–8586), a surprisingly genuine German restaurant that has high ceilings and long tables and features lots of sausage dishes on the menu. It's inexpensive and open daily, 11:30 A.M.–midnight.

After you've indulged your family's senses with Chinatown's foods, smells, and sights, head over to Boston's main shopping district, known as **Downtown Crossing.** The original **Filene's Basement** is in the basement of **Filene's,** naturally (426 Washington Street at Summer Street; 617 –357–2100). It's as good as you've heard—prices run the gamut from plain old mark-downs to rock-bottom—although the quality of the goods often suffers from overhandling. This isn't a place for small children or for anyone who isn't a die-hard shopper: Aisles can be narrow and shoppers downright rude, even to cute kids. Be wary of pickpockets. Open Monday through Saturday, 9:30 A.M.–7:00 P.M.; Sunday, noon–6:00 P.M.

Wander down the bricked-over section of busy **Washington Street,** a pedestrian zone, past lots of street vendors and performers, and you're likely to see a mounted police officer or two. They're accustomed to kids' questions and admiring glances, and the horses are very gentle, but do ask first before allowing your kids to pat the horses' noses.

At the corner of Washington and School streets is one of Boston's most beloved institutions, the **Globe Corner Bookstore** (1 School Street; 617–523–6658). Not only has the bookstore been in operation since 1828, but it's one of the most popular bookshops in a town that's known for its voracious readers. The store specializes in travel books, particularly New England–oriented travel, but you'll find a terrific children's section, too, as well as unique gift choices for the folks back home. The second floor is much roomier than the first. Open Monday through Saturday, 9:00 A.M.–6:00 P.M., and Sunday, noon–6:00 P.M.

Up Bromfield Street (from the Globe Corner Bookstore, backtrack along Washington Street a couple of blocks back; then turn right) is another good lunch spot, **Bruegger's Bagel Bakery** (32 Bromfield Street; 617–357–5577), where they bake the bagels right on the premises. Try one of their unusual cream cheese mixtures; the fresh berry varieties are particularly good. The homemade soups are excellent, too. You're not far from the Common here, so if it's a nice day, have your lunches wrapped up for a picnic. Open Monday through Saturday, 7:00 A.M.–6:00 P.M., and Sunday, 8:00 A.M.–5:00 P.M.

Jack's Joke Shop (172 Tremont Street; 617–426–9640) is a fun stop, especially if you have a family member who loves practical jokes. Buy 'em a warty nose, an extra finger, fake messes of various descriptions . . . you name it. Open Monday through Saturday, 8:30 A.M.–5:30 P.M.; closed Sunday.

COPLEY SQUARE AND THE BACK BAY

A short trip on the T is like an amusement park ride to a small child. Take the trip from **Park Street to Copley Square** and try to stand right up front, so the kids can see the tracks and look for the stations ahead. Fare is 85 cents per person for everyone over eleven, half-fare for kids between five and eleven, and free for the under-fives.

When you come out of the Copley Square T station, you'll surely look up—at the **John Hancock Tower.** If you remember the building's inauspicious introduction (just after its completion it began shedding windows, and several pedestrians were injured), don't worry; the windows were reengineered and replaced in 1977. The Hancock building is a sixty-two-story rhomboid, an unusual shape for a building and one that makes it change in appearance when you see it from different angles. From Copley Square it's a sharp, slim jab of reflective glass; from downtown it's a wide mirror for the older Hancock building next to it. The interior of the building is nothing like the exterior; the atmosphere is dreary and rather disappointing. But the real attraction of the tower is at its top. The sixtieth-floor **Observatory** (200 Clarendon Street; 617–247–1977) provides the most stunning views of Boston outside of a helicopter. Try to go on a clear day, when you may be able to see as far as Vermont. Open Monday through Saturday, 9:00 A.M.–11:00 P.M., and Sunday, noon–11:00 P.M. Admission is $3.50 for adults and $2.75 for kids five to fifteen.

It's hard to imagine now, but until 1857 this part of the city was a smelly tidal flat, fronted by a failed dam, called the Back Bay (Boston itself was actually a peninsula). By the mid-nineteenth century, the city had grown so much that the marshy tidal flats became an advantageous area for expansion and the landfill operation began. When it ended in 1890, the 450-acre area was crisscrossed with Boston's only grid system, and well over 1,000 new buildings had been built to house more people and businesses.

While you're in the Back Bay area, be sure to stroll over to **Commonwealth Avenue;** cross into the green area, called **Commonwealth Mall,** that runs from the Public Garden to the Fenway. You'll see other families here, mostly locals walking their dogs and stretching their legs. As you walk west (away from the Public Garden), note that the eight streets between here and Massachusetts Avenue are named in alphabetical order: Arlington, Berkeley, Clarendon, Dartmouth, Exeter, Fairfield, Gloucester, and Hereford.

Just around the corner from the Hancock Tower, the **Hard Rock Cafe** (131 Clarendon Street; 617–424–7625) brings in tourists by the handful (you're not likely to see many locals here). It's a fun place to have lunch—the burgers are excellent—and the kids will love it. Open daily, 11:00–2:00 A.M.

The **Back Bay Hilton** (40 Dalton Street; 800–874–0063 or 617–236–1100) is a big downtown hotel offering excellent family packages that include discount admission passes to many city attractions, a lending desk of children's books and videos, and a kids' menu in the hotel restaurant and through room service. Rates are very reasonable for a city hotel: $99–$139.

The teddy bear on the sidewalk in front of **F. A. O. Schwarz** (440 Boylston Street; 617–266–5101) is a favorite picture-taking site for families visiting Boston. Go inside to see the creative displays in the two-story toy store, and be sure to visit the book section.

Boston Ballet (19 Clarendon Street; 617–695–6950) is the largest dance center in New England. The Boston Ballet's version of *The Nutcracker* is the most popular in the country; tickets often sell out months in advance. One of the rehearsal studios is the same size as the Wang Center stage (where the troupe performs), which is one of the largest stages in the world. Tours are given Wednesday at 6:00 P.M. and Saturday at noon, year-round (during July and August you must make a reservation). *Note:* The **Wang Center** is at 270 Tremont Street. For Boston Ballet tickets call Ticketmaster at (617) 931–2000.

Boston Park Plaza Hotel (64 Arlington Street; 800–225–2008 or 617–426–2000) is a grande dame of a hotel that hosts many conventions and wedding receptions. A family package rate of $149 includes a room with two double beds and two bathrooms, complimentary parking, a story hour with milk and cookies, and a special late checkout for families with young kids who nap in the afternoon.

Newbury Street is Boston's boutique row. Designers' shops rule the roost here, though there are plenty of other businesses, running the gamut from art galleries to several excellent secondhand clothes shops. Whether or not you enjoy window shopping, it's also a nice street for walking, since the sidewalks are slightly wider and there are lots of sidewalk cafes that will tempt you to rest for a while over a drink or a light meal.

Waterstone's Booksellers (26 Exeter Street, corner of Newbury; 617–859–7300) is a three-story book-lover's heaven that took over the old Exeter Street Theatre Building several years ago. Story time in the children's book section is Sunday at 2:30 P.M.

At 248 Newbury Street is **Beacon Guest Houses** (617–266–7142), one of Boston's best-kept accommodations secrets. It's a small, no-nonsense place that's perfect if you're a self-sufficient type of family: They don't have TVs or room service, but they do have excellent rates and a superb location. If you know that you will spend more than a few days in Boston, call ahead to see whether they have an efficiency apartment for you.

Emack and Bolio's (290 Newbury Street; 617–247–8772) is a local chain of ice cream shops that specializes in unusual flavors created for loyal patrons who like to buy their treats in shops rather than out of a store freezer.

At the end of Newbury Street, on the left-hand corner of Newbury and Massachusetts Avenue, is the largest **Tower Records/Video** store in the country (360 Newbury Street; 617–247–5900). Teenagers love the place. Open Monday through Saturday, 9:00 A.M.–midnight, and Sunday, 11:00 A.M.–midnight.

HUNTINGTON AVENUE TO THE FENWAY

From the end of Newbury Street, walk across the Massachussetts Avenue bridge over the turnpike (there's a great view of the city skyline from here) and along Massachusetts Avenue, past the Berklee College of Music, and on for about 3 more blocks, until you see the enormous open area on the left. This, the international headquarters of the **Christian Science Church** (617–450–2000), contains several buildings of architectural note, including the 1894 Mother Church. The twenty-acre plaza incorporates a long reflecting pool, with a wonderful circular fountain at its eastern end. Your kids should feel free to pull off their shoes and wade; that's what it's there for. The plaza is a great place for the kids to work off any excess energy that they haven't lost during the day.

When the kids have satisfied themselves with the delights of running around in the plaza and splashing in the fountain, walk through the passageway between the Colonnade building and the church to the bronze-doored Christian Science Publishing Society (where the *Christian Science Monitor* is published) and, once inside, look for signs to the **Mapparium.** It's a 30-foot glass globe that you can walk into—one of the best geography lessons you'll ever see. Open Monday through Saturday, 9:30 A.M.–4:00 P.M.; closed Sunday. Free admission.

Symphony Hall (301 Massachusetts Avenue; 617–266–1492), home of the Boston Symphony Orchestra (popularly known as the BSO), is the most acoustically perfect auditorium in the United States. Tours are given as part of the BSO Youth Concert Series during the spring and fall. You must plan ahead if you wish to attend the series: The tickets go on sale each spring for the following fall/spring series (call the Youth Activities Office, 617–638–9375). If your family doesn't mind waiting in line in order to see a performance by one of the country's best symphony orchestras for a reasonable price, you can get same-day discounted tickets for the BSO on Tuesday, Thursday, and Friday by waiting in line at the box office: Arrive by 5:00 P.M. on Tuesday and Thursday and by 9:00 A.M. on Friday. If you want to order tickets by phone, call Symphony Charge (617–266–1200).

When your family is ready for another bout of museum-hopping (don't do it all in one day or you'll never have the energy for all the don't-miss exhibits), take the Green Line train marked E/Arborway and get off at the Museum/Ruggles stop on Huntington Avenue.

The **Museum of Fine Arts** (465 Huntington Avenue; 617–267–9300) is one of the country's great city museums, holding collections of fine art, antiquities, furniture, silver, and ceramics. Highlights include the Monet collection, recently rehung, and the nearby superb examples of work by Corot, Renoir, Manet, Pissaro, Gauguin, and van Gogh; the famous portraits of Sam Adams and Paul Revere by John Singleton Copley; several excellent portraits by John Singer Sargent; and mummies, altars, and hieroglyphics in the Egyptian rooms that are sure to satisfy the *Indiana Jones* fans in your family. Don't try to see the museum without a plan; you'll get lost and the kids will get bored. When you arrive, go to the Information Center and ask the staff about the day's family-oriented activities (there are usually several). If your family is particularly interested in seeing certain works of art, have a staff member mark the location on a map as well as the shortest way to get there. The museum shop is an excellent source of gifts and souvenirs; allow some time for this. Free coat check (do it; this will increase your family's comfort and lengthen your stay considerably). The entire museum is open on Tuesday and Thursday through

Sunday, 10:00 A.M.–5:00 P.M., and on Wednesday, 10:00 A.M.–10:00 P.M.; the West Wing only is open on Thursday and Friday, 5:00–10:00 P.M. All facilities are closed on Monday and most holidays. Free tours (with price of admission) are given on Tuesday through Friday at 10:30 A.M. and 1:30 P.M., on Wednesday at 6:15 P.M., and on Saturday at 11:00 A.M. and 1:30 P.M. Admission is $7.00 for adults, $3.50 for kids ages six to seventeen, and free on Wednesday after 4:00 P.M.

If you ask ten museum-loving Bostonians the question, "If I'm going to see only one museum in Boston, what should I see?" it's likely that at least eight of them will answer, "The Gardner Museum." The **Isabella Stewart Gardner Museum** (280 The Fenway; 617–566–1401) was the home of Mrs. Gardner, who built the beautiful building, called Fenway Court, to house her personal art collection. A New York native (1840–1924), Gardner was a most unusual woman who shocked Boston with her short-sleeved dresses and her unorthodox habits (she was reported to have walked her pet lions down Beacon Street, on leashes, like poodles). Her legacy to her adopted city is this museum, a building that is as much a work of art as the treasures it holds. The 1903 Venetian-style palazzo building's heart is a glass-ceilinged, three-story courtyard that holds a lovely indoor garden. When Gardner died in 1924, she left a will that turned the house into a museum with specific instructions that absolutely *nothing* could ever be changed. Therefore, every painting and sculpture and piece of furniture is in the same spot where she chose to place it, nearly a hundred years ago. Much of the art collection is from the Italian Renaissance and Dutch seventeenth-century master period, but there are several fine late nineteenth-century pieces, too, notably the portrait of Mrs. Gardner painted by her friend John Singer Sargent and a beautiful small seascape by James McNeill Whistler. Despite the grandness of the building and the breathtaking art collection, the museum's staff manages to preserve the museum's origins as a private home: Flowers and plants are tastefully placed throughout the museum, a cat prowls the house, and staff members talk of Mrs. Gardner as if she were still in charge. Art-loving families should budget at least a half-day to explore the museum. To keep their interest, suggest to the kids that they keep an eye out for the museum cat, or that they try to spot the animals in many of the paintings and sculptures. Open

Tuesday through Sunday, 11:00 a.m.–5:00 p.m. Tours on Thursday and Friday at 2:30 p.m. and sometimes on other days, too; ask when you arrive. Admission is $6.00 for adults, $3.00 for students, and free for kids under twelve; free admission on Wednesday.

Just a few blocks and yet a world away from Mrs. Gardner's palazzo is **Fenway Park** (4 Yawkey Way; 617–267–1700 for tickets and 267–8661 for the info line), home of the **Boston Red Sox.** Even after a recent refurbishment, it's still a bit rickety, but its size (smallest in the Major League) and genuine old-time charm make it the best place in the country to watch a baseball game. The bleachers are the least expensive part of the park, but you may get stuck by a group of loud beer-swilling (and-spilling) fans; it's best to try to buy box seats. Since you're never far from the field, there's not a bad seat in the house. The box office is open 9:00 A.M.–5:00 P.M. When you call for tickets, ask whether there are any upcoming family days; the discounts can be well worth the wait.

Wheelock Family Theatre (180 The Riverway, Boston; 617–734–4760) performs family-oriented musicals and plays from October through May on Friday night, Saturday afternoon and evening, and Sunday afternoon. The theater has an excellent reputation for unusual productions and nontraditional casting. Reservations required.

BIKING IN BOSTON AND CAMBRIDGE

One of the city's many fine green spaces is the **Charles River Reservation** (for information call the Metropolitan District Commission, 617–727–5250), which borders the Charles, in both Boston and Cambridge, from Science Park all the way up to Harvard. A nice **riverside bike ride** (or a long walk for an energetic family) begins on the Boston side at the Community Boating boathouse, next to Massachusetts General Hospital. Continue along the riverside area called the **Esplanade,** which runs below Beacon Hill and the Back Bay, past the **Hatch Shell.** This is where the Boston Pops perform free concerts during the summer (their Fourth of July concert regularly attracts 300,000 people) and, on summer Friday evenings, it's where free movies are shown (imagine several thousand people gathered on blankets to watch *The Wizard of Oz* outdoors; it's fun).

You'll find several good playgrounds in this area, too. Continue along past the lagoon up to the bridge at Massachusetts Avenue (just to confuse you, this bridge is called the Harvard Bridge).

On the Cambridge side ride along the Charles between MIT and Harvard. On Sundays during daylight saving time (approximately April through October), Memorial Drive is closed to auto traffic between the Western Avenue Bridge and the Eliot Bridge. Memorial Drive fills with walkers, strollers, bikers, skateboarders, and in-line skaters.

CAMBRIDGE

As home to two of the country's most illustrious universities, Harvard and MIT, bustling Cambridge owes much of its vibrance to the students, faculty, and staff of those fine institutions, who are ruthless judges of food, bookstores, museums, art galleries, fashion, film, and the performing arts. As a result, the cultural life in this relatively small city is as good as that in any other city in America.

As a destination for families, Cambridge will be more interesting to those with teenagers. You'll find enough shopping in and around Harvard Square to satisfy the most demanding teenager, and the range of food will thrill everyone. Don't leave Cambridge without walking through **Harvard Yard,** or without stepping down to the Charles River and at least to the center of the graceful **Weeks Bridge,** or without driving along Massachusetts Avenue until you reach MIT. These places give you the essence of the flavor of Cambridge.

Do yourself a favor and leave the car in a garage; parking is nearly impossible to find, and if you're lucky enough to find a spot, you'll have to keep running back to feed quarters into the meter (Cambridge meter maids have a sixth sense about every meter that runs out, and they are impervious to protests).

The best place to begin a trip to Cambridge is, of course, **Harvard Square,** where, regardless of the weather, you'll see packs of teenagers riding skateboards, zipping around corners and over low walls on in-line skates, and just hanging out. The street life is rather more interesting across the street, in the wide pedestrian area between Brattle Street and Mt. Auburn Street; musicians and other performers are encouraged to play here, and sometimes they're pretty good (tell the kids that this is where the musician Tracy Chapman got her start). On a warm afternoon it's nice to sit on the brick walls that were designed for that purpose, have a snack, and let the street life entertain the family for a while.

Voracious readers will enjoy bookstore-hopping in Harvard Square. The best is **Wordsworth** (30 Brattle Street; 617–354–5201), with the **Harvard Book Shop** (1256 Massachusetts Avenue; 617–661–1515) running a close second. Other Harvard Square bookstores include the **Globe Corner Bookstore** (49 Palmer Street, 617–497–6277), an annex of the downtown shop, which specializes in travel books; **Barillari's** (1 Mifflin Place; 617–864–2400), with a good children's section and a cafe; **Schoenhof's** (76A Mt. Auburn Street; 617–547–8855), for foreign books; and the **Starr Book Company** (29 Plympton; 617–547–6864), for used textbooks and great atmosphere (it's in the funky building that houses the *Harvard Lampoon* offices).

Another don't-miss store in Harvard Square is **HMV** (1 Brattle Street; 617–868–9696), an enormous music store with an especially good selection of classical and jazz recordings.

LearningSmith (25 Brattle Street; 617–661–6008), operated by Boston's topnotch public television station, WGBH, its one of the most innovative toy/book/gadget stores you'll ever see; just try to leave without playing with something.

For clothes-hound teenagers this area is home to many excellent clothing shops, including **Jasmine and Sola** (37 Brattle Street; 617–354 –6043), **Urban Outfitters** (11 John F. Kennedy Street; 617–864–0070), **Allston Beat** (36 John F. Kennedy Street; 617–868–0316), **Serendipity** (1312 Massachusetts Avenue; 617–661–7143), and, a few blocks farther down Massachusetts Avenue, **Oona's Experienced Clothing** (1210 Massachusetts Avenue; 617–491–2654), one of Cambridge's best secondhand stores (another is the **Garment District,** (200 Broadway; 617–876–5230).

When you're shopped out, walk down John F. Kennedy Street to the river (be careful crossing Memorial Drive). The wide grassy area is great for running around, picnicking, and watching the pleasure craft go by. You'll see the Radcliffe and Harvard boathouses here, and if you're lucky, a few oarsmen and -women will carry their sculls out to the river while you're watching. Walk along the river inland and you'll pass the graceful sycamore trees that line Memorial Drive.

Before you leave the Harvard Square area of Cambridge, do take the time to walk into **Harvard Yard.** It's a bit of early America that's been beautifully preserved and lovingly used since the early eighteenth century. Harvard was founded in 1636, but none of these buildings date from that period.

Near the Yard is **Bartley's Burger Cottage** (1246 Massachusetts Avenue; 617–354–6559), which, as the name suggests, features burgers and other simple fare. Students congregate here for the large helpings and low prices; out-of-towners and alumni bask in the collegiate atmosphere. *Note:* The eatery has no bathrooms.

Just a few blocks away is **Herrell's Ice Cream** (15 Dunster Street; 617–497–2179), opened by Steve Herrell after he sold his wildly success-ful chain, Steve's.

If your family likes real Southern barbecue, **Red Bones** (55 Chester Street in Somerville; 617–628–2200) is a great place to venture for dinner. The ambience is friendly and noisy, so families won't feel out of place, and the food is cooked over a hot hickory fire.

Margaret's Bed and Breakfast (75 Wendell Street, Cambridge; 617–876–3450) is a cozy three-room B & B in a quiet neighborhood just north of the Harvard campus.

Mt. Auburn Cemetery (580 Mt. Auburn Street; 617–547–7105) may sound like a strange place for a picnic. When you arrive there, you'll see why so many Cambridge and Boston families make this a weekend des-tination: Its 164 acres are planted with 1,000 varieties of trees, shrubs, flowers, and other plants. This was the first garden cemetery in America when it was founded in 1831; the best time to visit is during the spring, when it seems as though every plant is in bloom. Stop at the office at the main gate (open Monday through Saturday, 8:30 A.M.–4:00 P.M.) for a map and ask about today's special activities, such as free guided walks to the resting places of the cemetery's more famous residents (Henry Wadsworth Longfellow, Isabella Stewart Gardner, and Winslow Homer, to name a few) and horticultural tours.

Located in a mall next to the Charles River, not far from MIT, is the **Sports Museum of New England** (Cambridgeside Galleria; 617–787-7678). The most satisfied visitors are kids who follow the Red Sox, Celtics, or Bruins, but enthusiastic sports fans will probably enjoy looking at the collections of memorabilia, such as one-hundred-year-old baseball spikes and the life-size carved statues of Boston idols Larry Bird, Carl Yastrzemski, and Bobby Orr. Budget some time to watch several of the videos of big-game highlights. Hours are Monday through Saturday, 9:30 A.M.–10:00 P.M., and Sunday, noon–6:00 P.M.

Straddling a dam at the mouth of the Charles River, the **Museum of Science** (Science Park; 617–723–2500) deserves its reputation as a favorite field trip for Boston-area schoolkids. The museum is enormous; think about bringing a stroller if you have toddlers. Young kids may not want to leave the Discovery Center, which was designed (and recently renovated) with them in mind. Other favorite exhibits include the Transparent Woman, which lights up to display organs; the Live Animal Show; and the Special Effects Stage, where, with the help of audiovisual technology, you can fly over Boston or walk on the moon. The **Omni Theater** and the **Hayden Planetarium** are run separately; if you want to see exhibits as well as one (or both) of these attractions, you'll have to buy combination tickets. Buy your Omni tickets early, since it often sells out early, especially on winter weekends. From Memorial Day through Labor Day, the museum is open 9:00 A.M.–7:00 P.M., Monday through Thursday and Saturday and Sunday, and 9:00 A.M.–9:00 P.M. Friday. Between Labor Day and Memorial Day, the museum is open 9:00 A.M.–5:00 P.M. Monday through Thursday and Saturday and Sunday (free on Wednesday afternoon), and 9:00 A.M.–9:00 P.M. Friday.

CHARLESTOWN

The **Charlestown Navy Yard** (Constitution Road, Charlestown; 617–242-5601) is an on-site memorial to the thousands of warships that were built here between 1800 and 1974. For kids the highlight is a visit to the **USS *Constitution.*** "Old Ironsides," as it's known (for its resilience rather than its materials; it's an all-wood ship), began its service in 1797; it's still commissioned, though it leaves the dock only once a year. The tour of the

A tour of the USS Constitution *will make history come alive.*
(Courtesy Department of the Navy)

triple-decked ship, given by crew members, runs approximately twenty-five minutes and is well worth planning for (try to arrive early in the day to avoid being part of a too-large group). While you're at the Navy Yard, don't miss the wonderful **playground at Shipyard Park** (beyond the USS *Constitution* Museum), which features a shiplike climbing structure. Winter hours for the USS *Constitution* are Monday through Friday, 10:00 A.M.–4:00 P.M., and Saturday and Sunday, 9:00 A.M.–5:00 P.M.; spring and fall hours are daily, 9:00 A.M.–5:00 P.M.; summer hours are daily, 9:00 A.M.–6:00 P.M.

In the center of Charlestown, the **Bunker Hill Monument** rises from the spot where, in June 1775, Colonel William Prescott told his revolutionary militia, "Don't one of you fire until you see the whites of their eyes." As most schoolchildren know, the British eventually won the battle, but not until they had lost well over 1,000 soldiers to Prescott's brave band; the battle was an effective morale booster to the revolutionaries in the early days of the war. Climb the grassy hill, which is actually called Breed's Hill (the Bunker part of the name comes from the bunker that the colonists built atop the hill), to reach the base of the monument, which you can climb (295 winding steps, about a fifteen-minute climb; not an appropriate ascent for small kids or for parents who don't want to carry them most of the way). The museum called the **Bunker Hill Pavilion** (617–241–7575), at the monument's base, has good dioramas of the battle. The monument is open daily, 9:00 A.M.–4:30 P.M., except for Thanksgiving, Christmas, and New Year's Day. The museum is open 9:00 A.M.–5:00 P.M. Free admission to both.

LEXINGTON AND CONCORD

Just a few miles to the northwest of Cambridge are the historic towns of Lexington and Concord. The "shot heard round the world" was fired in Lexington, and the subsequent first battles of the War for Independence were fought there and in Concord. During the nation's first century, Concord attracted thinkers and writers such as Nathaniel Hawthorne, Ralph Waldo Emerson, Louisa May Alcott, and Henry David Thoreau, whose homes are now open to the public. Thoreau's beloved Walden Pond is a terrific spot to learn a little about Thoreau or to picnic, sun, and swim. And the DeCordova Museum and Sculpture Park is another great picnic spot as well as an innovative contemporary art museum.

Begin your family's trip to Concord at the **Old North Bridge** (Monument Street). This is the spot where the "shot heard round the world" was fired. The current bridge is actually the fourth reproduction since the historic event. Nearby (a ten-minute walk) is the **Battle Road Visitor Center** (171 Liberty Street, Concord; 508–369–6993) at the Minute Man National Historical Park Headquarters, where your family can watch an interesting short video about the events of April 19, 1775, and look at a diorama of the battle area. The center is open from April through December, daily, 8:30 A.M.–5:00 P.M. Park rangers answer questions at the center and also provide good presentations at the bridge itself (from June to October, daily; spring and fall, weekends only; winter, by advance request only).

In Lexington **Battle Green** (1875 Massachusetts Avenue, Lexington; 617–862–1450) is the site of the first battle of the war. The visitor center has a diorama of the Battle of Lexington as well as an interesting display of recently excavated artifacts from the battle.

Minute Man National Historical Park is a long, narrow park that extends along Battle Road from Lexington to Lincoln to Concord. It was established to commemorate the events that took place along the winding, hilly road on April 19, 1775. Unless your family knows a lot of minute details about the battles, you'll probably most enjoy walking up the path that approaches the bridge. There's a nice 1-mile walk (follow the markers) to the ruins of the **Fiske House,** a farmhouse that was in the midst of the battle area.

Near the middle of Concord is **Orchard House** (399 Lexington Road, Concord; 508–369–4118), home of *Little Women* author Louisa May Alcott and her family. The house museum is remarkably homey and informal; there are no ropes or fences, and there are enough recognizable items on view to make Alcott's fans feel as though she and her sisters have just left the room. Be sure to take the tour here. Hours April through October are Monday through Saturday, 10:00 A.M.–4:30 P.M., and Sunday, 1:00–4:30 P.M.; hours November through March are Saturday, 10:00 A.M.–4:30 P.M., and Sunday, 1:00–4:30 P.M. Admission is $4.00 for adults, $3.50 for kids thirteen to eighteen, and $2.50 for kids six to twelve; family rates are available.

Longfellow's Wayside Inn (Boston Post Road, Sudbury; 508–443–8846) is a historic inn that's also a pleasant place to spend a night.

Learn all about the Revolutionary War as you tour Lexington and Concord.
(Courtesy Greater Merrimack Valley Convention and Visitors Bureau)

The red clapboard building, the oldest operating inn in the country, was built in 1702; the Ford Foundation bought it and renovated it in the early 1920s. There are ten guest rooms, two of them (original to the house) reached by a narrow old staircase, and all with private bath. The dining room is a popular restaurant that serves breakfast, lunch, and dinner (reservations required for dinner). On the Wayside Inn's one-hundred-acre grounds is the **Red Schoolhouse,** famous as the school that Mary and her little lamb attended; the Ford Foundation moved the building here from nearby Sterling, Massachusetts, during the 1920s renovation project (the schoolhouse is open daily during the summer, noon–5:00 P.M.).

The **DeCordova Museum and Sculpture Park** (Sandy Pond Road, Lincoln; 617–259–8355), housed in the castlelike brick mansion of a wealthy, early twentieth-century Boston businessman, is dedicated to promoting appreciation of contemporary art by American artists, particularly those working in the New England area. An ambitious schedule of exhibitions attracts a large, loyal audience. Outdoors on the museum's beautiful grounds, the sculpture park features permanent and temporary sculptures, some of which are musical and most of which will intrigue the kids. During the summer a fine concert series called Art in the Park is held in the outdoor amphitheater. Otherwise, the DeCordova's year-round hours are Tuesday through Friday, 10:00 A.M.–5:00 P.M., and weekends, noon–5:00 P.M. Gallery admission is $4.00; admission to the sculpture park is free.

Walden Pond State Reservation (Route 126, Concord; 508–369–3284) can be a crowded place, especially when the water is warm enough for swimming. It's best to come here in the off-season; otherwise, it's hard to imagine the peace that Thoreau found when he lived here alone. His cabin burned down long ago, but in its place is a large pile of rocks that visitors have placed here as a simple tribute. Open daily after Memorial Day to Labor Day, 8:00 A.M.–7:00 P.M.; open weekends from mid-May through Memorial Day and from Labor Day through Columbus Day, 8:00 A.M.–7:00 P.M.

Just a few miles to the west, in South Lincoln, **Drumlin Farm** (South Great Road, South Lincoln; 617–259–9807) is a magnet for Boston-area families with young children. It's the headquarters for the Massachusetts Audubon Society as well as a "demonstration farm," which means that the exhibits are built around what you might find on a typical New England farm: kitchen gardens, flower gardens, grapevines, meadows, ponds, and, of course, lots of animals, including cows, pigs, horses, birds, and forest creatures, too. Excellent kid-oriented tours, discussions, and walks are given on weekends at 11:00 A.M. and noon. *Note:* Picnicking is allowed in designated areas only, and please don't bring dogs here. Open year-round, Tuesday through Friday and on holidays (except Thanksgiving, Christmas, and New Year's Day), 9:00 A.M.–5:00 P.M. Admission is $5.00 for adults, $3.50 for kids three to fifteen, and free for kids under three.

The **Minuteman Bike Path** is a fun way to travel from northern Cambridge through Arlington, Lexington, and Bedford. It's an 11-mile path that begins at the Alewife station in Cambridge (the northernmost stop on the Red Line) and follows some unused railroad tracks, ending in suburban Bedford. For more information about this trail and others in the Boston area, contact the Department of Environmental Management, 100 Cambridge Street, Boston 02202 (617–727–3180).

JAMAICA PLAIN AND BROOKLINE

Brookline is a separate city in government only; everything else about it is very much part of Boston city life. To the south of Brookline, Jamaica Plain is part of Boston proper.

The Tropical Rain Forest and the Children's Zoo are the highlights of the seventy-two acre **Franklin Park Zoo** (Franklin Park; 617–442–2002), which is undergoing a long-term revitalization program along with the enormous Franklin Park. The three-acre rain forest is the largest of its kind in North America. It holds hippopotamuses, gorillas, big cats, crocodiles, and thousands of exotic birds. The Children's Zoo has a petting barn where kids can get acquainted with farm animals, such as cows, donkeys, and sheep. At the Hooves and Horns area, your children can explain the differences between camels and dromedaries (why is it that most kids know this?) and see zebras and wallabies. Open spring through fall, Monday through Friday, 9:00 A.M.–4:00 P.M., and Saturday, Sunday, and holidays, 10:00 A.M.–6:00 P.M. Admission is $5.00 for adults, $2.50 for kids ages four to eleven, and free for kids ages three and

KELLY'S TOP ANNUAL EVENTS IN GREATER BOSTON

Chinese New Year, late January or early February, Chinatown, Boston; (617) 536–1400

New England Boat Show, February, Bayside Exposition Center, Boston; (617) 536–1400

New England Flower Show, March, Bayside Exposition Center, Boston; (617) 536–9280

St. Patrick's Day Parade, March 17, South Boston; (617) 536–1400

Boston Marathon, Patriots Day (the third Monday of April), Hopkinton to Boston; (617) 435–6905

Paul Revere and Billy Dawes's Ride Reenactment, Patriots Day, Boston to Lexington; (617) 862–1450

Battle of Lexington and Concord Reenactment, Patriots Day, Lexington; (617) 861–0928

Big Apple Circus, April, Boston; (617) 426–8855

Ducklings Day, the last Sunday of April, Boston Public Garden; (617) 426–1885

Lilac Sunday, May, Arnold Arboretum, Jamaica Plain; (617) 524–1718

Art Newbury Street, May, Boston; (617) 267–7961

Kite Festival, May, Franklin Park, Jamaica Plain; (617) 725–4505

Bunker Hill Day, June 17, Charlestown; (617) 242–5628

Art in the Park, June, DeCordova Museum, Lincoln; (617) 259–8355

Harborfest, July, Boston; (617) 227–1528

Feste (saints' festivals), nearly every weekend in July and August, the North End; (617) 536–4100

Boston Pops Fourth of July Concert, July 4, Esplanade, Boston

USS *Constitution* Turnaround, July 4, Charlestown Navy Yard, Charlestown; (617) 242–5601

U.S. Pro Tennis Championship, August, Longwood Tennis Club, Chestnut Hill; (617) 731–4500

Head of the Charles Regatta, October, Cambridge/Boston; (617) 864–8415

The Nutcracker, November through early January, Boston Ballet, Boston; (617) 931–2000

Christmas Tree Lighting, late November, Prudential Center, Boston.

Black Nativity, December; (617) 442–8614

Boston Tea Party Reenactment, December, Old South Meeting House to Boston Harbor; (617) 338–1773

First Night, December 31, Boston; (617) 542–1399

under; admission is free 10:00 A.M.–11:00 A.M. Sunday and 9:00–10:00 A.M. Tuesday. Call for directions and parking instructions.

In the Brookline Village neighborhood is an outstanding bookstore, the **Children's Bookshop** (238 Washington Street, Brookline Village; 617–734–7323). The superb selection and knowledgeable staff are reason enough to visit, but do call ahead to find out what's coming up in the popular reading program by local and famous authors and illustrators.

A pleasant family outing can be had at **Larz Anderson Park,** a sixty-acre park in Brookline. Housed in a gorgeous 1888 carriage house that looks for all the world like a castle, the **Museum of Transportation** (Carriage House, Larz Anderson Park, 15 Newton Street, Brookline; 617–522–6140) boasts an impressive collection of restored antique carriages, classic cars, and trolleys, as well as an aggressive special-exhibit schedule of such shows as "Cars of the Stars." Open year-round, Wednesday through Sunday, 10:00 A.M.–5:00 P.M. Admission is $4.00 for adults, $2.00 for children three to twelve, and free for kids under three.

On the hill behind the museum is a wonderful picnic spot that is also one of the best kite-flying hills in Greater Boston. Off to the left at the bottom of the hill are soccer fields and a baseball diamond, much used by Brookline's many families. Next to the playing fields is a great playground with a twisty slide and an unusual seesaw made from old telephone poles. Continue on past the playground down the hill to the duck pond and more choice picnicking sites.

DORCHESTER

The **John F. Kennedy Library and Museum** (Columbia Point, Dorchester; 617–929–4500) is the busiest of all the presidential libraries. The library itself is rarely visited by tourists, however; for most visitors the attraction here is the museum's excellent exhibition program about JFK and RFK, complete with reminiscences taped by the late Rose Fitzgerald Kennedy as well as several close friends of the Kennedy clan. The building itself, designed by I. M. Pei and completed in 1979, is an extraordinary sight from the expressway: Its sweeping shape captures JFK's love of the ocean and of sailing. Open daily, 9:00 A.M.–5:00 P.M., year-round, except Thanksgiving, Christmas, and New Year's Day. Admission is $5.00 for adults, $1.00 for kids six and older, and free for under-sixes.

Combine a trip to the JFK Museum with a tour of *The Boston Globe* (135 Morrissey Boulevard, Dorchester; 617–929–2653). Find out what's involved in publishing a daily newspaper, watch the presses publishing in action, and ask lots of questions. The ninety-minute tours are given on Tuesday and Thursday. *Note:* Reservations are required, and children must be at least twelve. Free.

QUINCY

Just a few miles south of Boston proper is Quincy, which has the unique claim to fame of being both the birthplace and the burial place of two U.S. presidents: John Adams, the second president, and his son John Quincy Adams, the sixth president.

The **Adams National Historic Site** (135 Adams Street, Quincy, 617–773–1177), run by the National Park Service, is the house and gardens of the Adams family. When John and Abigail Adams moved here in 1787, fifty-six years after the house was built, there were only seven rooms. As their fortune grew, they expanded the house until it had twenty rooms. Of special note here are the cathedral-ceilinged library, with its 12,000-volume collection of Adams family books, and the study where John Adams died on July 4, 1826, coincidentally the same day that Thomas Jefferson died, fifty years to the day after the Declaration of Independence, which the two men drafted together, was signed. Do take the excellent Park Service-led tour of the house. Here also are the small saltbox houses where the Adams presidents were born, the **John Adams and John Quincy Adams Birthplaces** (1250 Hancock Street, Quincy; 617–770–1175). The historic site and the birthplaces are open mid-April through mid-November, daily, 9:00 A.M.–5:00 P.M. Admission is $2.00. *Note:* You can visit the birthplaces only as part of a guided tour, which lasts approximately one hour.

The **United First Parish Church** (1306 Hancock Street, Quincy) holds the remains of the two Adams presidents and their wives.

If your family is hungry for lunch while you're in Quincy, visit **La Paloma** (195 Newport Avenue; 617–773–9512), which consistently wins awards as "Best Mexican Restaurant" in the metropolitan Boston area. The recognition is well deserved, and prices are very reasonable.

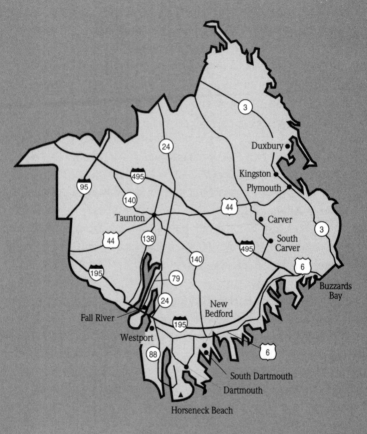

Duxbury

Kingston
Plymouth

24

495

95

140

Taunton

44

138

Carver

44

South
Carver

3

140

495

6

79

Buzzards
Bay

24

New
Bedford

195

Fall River

Westport

88

6

South Dartmouth

Dartmouth

Horseneck Beach

Plymouth and the South Shore

Plymouth and the South Shore

More than a million tourists pass through "America's Hometown" each year, and for good reason. The *Mayflower II,* Plymouth Rock, and Plimoth Plantation tell the well-known story of our country's first permanent European settlers vividly, with only minor embellishments. Of the many tourist attractions that are packed into this tiny town, the rock, the boat, and the outdoor museum are by far the most interesting to kids. If you can, try to visit Plymouth during the spring or late fall—Thanksgiving is best, of course—when there are fewer tour buses.

DUXBURY AND KINGSTON

Heading south of Boston during the summer? Don't miss **Duxbury Beach** (at the end of Route 139, accessed through the Green Harbor section of Marshfield, 617–837–3112). This 5-mile-long stretch of sand and beach grass is one of the finest barrier beaches along the Atlantic Coast, and its old-fashioned, full-service bathhouse is a great find for car-bound travelers. For a quarter you can stow your clothes in a basket, spend the day on the beach, and then wash the sand and salt water off the kids (and yourselves) before you return to the car. There's a good snack bar, too. Lifeguards are on duty from late May through early September. Parking is $8.00 on weekends, $7.00 on weekdays.

On your way to or from Duxbury Beach, drive or walk across the **Powder Point Bridge,** the longest wooden bridge on the East Coast. The pedestrian portion of the bridge is plenty wide, allowing room for walkers to pass behind the fishing enthusiasts who gather along the bridge.

On the way back from the beach, stop at **Farfar's Danish Ice Cream Shop** (Millbrook Station, St. George's Road, Duxbury). The owners make all their delicious ice cream daily on the premises (a converted train depot). Sit inside if it's hot outside, or else enjoy the large deck out back.

On the way south to Plymouth, the town of Kingston has several family-style restaurants, the best of which is **Persy's Place** (117 Main Street/Route 3A, Kingston; 617–585–5464). Persy's claims to have New England's largest breakfast menu. Whether or not they do, every member of the family will certainly find something that appeals, from plain toast to catfish on eggs. The portions are generous, the prices are reasonable, and the decor is similar to that of an old-fashioned country store. Open daily for breakfast and lunch.

PLYMOUTH

When you arrive in Plymouth, your first stop should be one of the two excellent tourist information centers. Adjacent to the highway, the **Massachusetts Tourist Information Center** (exit 5 on Route 3 South; 508–746–1150 or 746–1152) carries an excellent selection of books, maps, and brochures. The parking lot is plenty large, and there are clean rest rooms and picnic tables. The hard-to-stump staff is happy to answer your questions and point you in the right direction, either in person or over the phone. Open year-round, daily, 8:45 A.M.–5:00 P.M. The **Plymouth Visitor Information Center/Discover Plymouth** (Water Street; 508–747–7525 or 800–872–1620) is smaller than the highway-side information center, but it's located right at the waterfront, near most of the sites your family came to Plymouth to see. The selection of tourist literature is good here, the staff is helpful, and the rest rooms are conveniently located (baby-changing stations in both). From April through December open daily, 9:00 A.M.–5:00 P.M.; from June through August open daily, 9:00 A.M.–9:00 P.M.

For families with very young children, or families who would rather see everything quickly without having to do too much walking, the **Plymouth Rock Trolley** (22 Main Street, Plymouth; 508–747–3419) is a convenient way to get around. The trolley stops at all the major sites, from Plymouth

KELLY'S TOP FAMILY ADVENTURES IN PLYMOUTH AND THE SOUTH SHORE

1. Plimoth Plantation, Plymouth
2. *Mayflower II,* Plymouth
3. Duxbury Beach, Marshfield/Duxbury
4. New Bedford Whaling Museum, New Bedford
5. Battleship Cove and the Fall River Carousel, Fall River
6. Horseneck State Beach, Westport

Rock to the *Mayflower II,* during each forty-five-minute trip. For the price of one ticket per person, you can get on and off the trolley as many times as you like. During the summer the trolley ride is extended to Plimoth Plantation and Long Beach. Operates daily from early May through Thanksgiving weekend, 9:00 A.M.–5:00 P.M., and until 8:00 P.M. during the summer. Tickets are $6.00 for adults and $3.00 for kids.

Another fun trip is the **boat ride from Plymouth to Provincetown,** where the *Mayflower* band stopped briefly in 1620 before continuing on to Plymouth. The *Cape Cod Clipper* (State Pier; 800–242–2469) operates daily from late May through late September. It's a ninety-minute ride across chilly Cape Cod Bay—which is twice as long as it would take you to drive there. Reservations are strongly recommended. Fares run $22.00 for adults, $14.00 for kids under twelve, and $2.00 for bikes.

If your family would prefer to take a boat ride to nowhere in particular, call Captain John Lifrieri (508–746–3688), who gives morning, afternoon, and sunset cruises on his 41-foot sloop, the **Jehovah Jireh,** out of Plymouth Town Pier. The price is $22–$34 per person.

Once you've visited the tourist information center and planned your day, head for **Plymouth Rock** (on Water Street). As any schoolchild in America can tell you, the story is that the first European settlers in Plymouth stepped off the *Mayflower* onto this rock in 1620. Considering its prominence in American history, the size of the rock may disappoint you; it's a rather ordinary-looking boulder. Nevertheless, it's the number-one tourist attraction in Plymouth.

Down the hill from Plymouth Rock is the ***Mayflower II*** (State Pier, 508–746–1622), a reproduction of the original boat that brought the Pilgrims from England to Plymouth. The tours are highly recommended; the Pilgrim-costumed staff knows all sorts of facts about the boat, which seems astonishingly small when you think about the 102 people who crowded onto it during its first journey from England to America. The *Mayflower II* is usually open, though it makes occasional trips to other New England destinations each summer. Admission is $5.75 for adults, $3.75 for kids five to twelve, and free for kids under five; special rates if you visit the boat and Plimoth Plantation on the same day.

Three miles south of "downtown" Plymouth is one of New England's best living museums, **Plimoth Plantation** (Route 3A/Warren Avenue; 508–746–1622). Budget at least half a day to see this remarkable reproduction of a 1627 Pilgrim village; it is populated by authentically costumed people who play, convincingly, the parts of the residents. Ask them questions about their clothes, their chores, what they do for fun, what they eat, how they survive without indoor plumbing—whatever comes to mind. The best day of the year to visit the plantation is Thanksgiving, of course; call ahead to make a meal reservation. The gift shop has a large stock of books about Plymouth and the Pilgrims' lives and times. Open April through November, daily, 9:00 A.M.–5:00 P.M. Admission is $15.00 for adults, $9.00 for kids five to twelve, and free for kids under five; special rates if you visit the *Mayflower II* and Plimoth Plantation on the same day.

In operation since 1824, **Pilgrim Hall Museum** (75 Court Street, Plymouth; 508–746–1620) holds the largest existing collection of Pilgrim possessions, including a portion of the *Sparrow-Hawk,* one of the ships that brought the earliest European migrants to Plymouth. The only known

Be sure to allow for plenty of time to explore Plimoth Plantation. (Photo by Ted Curtin)

contemporaneous painting of a *Mayflower* passenger, Edward Winslow, is here, too. Open daily, 9:30 A.M.–4:30 P.M.

To learn about something other than Pilgrims, visit **Cranberry World** (225 Water Street, Plymouth; 508–746–2350). Ocean Spray sponsors this free center of information about cranberries, which includes a scaled-down reproduction of a cranberry bog, among other exhibits, and lots of free samples. Open May through November.

The Children's Museum of Plymouth (46–48 Main Street, Plymouth, 508–747–1234) is not your usual children's museum; this one allows kids to operate pint-sized versions of several elements of everyday life in contemporary Plymouth, such as deejaying at the radio station, operating a weather station at the lighthouse, riding on a fire engine, and making doughnuts at Plymouth's Dunkin' Donuts franchise. From mid-April through Labor Day, open daily; from Labor Day through mid-April, open weekends, holidays, and during school vacations.

Plymouth National Wax Museum (16 Carver Street, Plymouth; 508–746–6468) will probably seem cheesy to the grown-ups, but kids love the life-size wax figures of prominent Plymouth residents. Open daily from March through December. Admission is $5.50 for adults, $2.00 for kids five to twelve, and free for kids under five.

The **Mayflower Society Museum** (42 Summer Street, Plymouth; 508–746–2259) is housed in a beautiful white building with a sweeping double staircase and a mother lode of history: The original owner of the house (built in 1754) was Edward Winslow, who fled to Canada along with other Tories when the War for Independence began; the author and transcendentalist Ralph Waldo Emerson was married in the front parlor in 1835; and seven years later ether was discovered here. Call ahead if you're interested in researching your family's history; the building is the headquarters of the General Society of Mayflower Descendants, who have extensive archives and libraries of information that are open to the public (for a fee).

Plymouth has many **historic houses** that are open to the public; among these are two that tend to capture kids' interest more than the others.

Built in 1640, the **Richard Sparrow House** (42 Summer Street; 508–747–1240) is now Plymouth's oldest surviving wooden frame house.

The sparsely furnished house gives visitors a view of early Pilgrim life in an authentic setting. Donations requested.

The **Jabez Howland House** (33 Sandwich Street; 508–746–9490) is the only surviving house in Plymouth that is known to have been inhabited by *Mayflower* passengers. Soon after they landed in Plymouth in 1620, John Howland and Elizabeth Tilley married. They had ten children. Their youngest son, Jabez, purchased the house from its original owners in the late 1660s. Thereafter the parents lived with Jabez and his family during the winter months in order to be close to their church. After John died in 1673 (he was eighty), Elizabeth lived in the house with Jabez until she died. Nearly 300 years later, the John Howland Society (made up of Howland descendants) conducted a thorough restoration of the house, then furnished it with period furniture. Open late May through mid-October and on Thanksgiving weekend, 10:00 A.M.–4:30 P.M.

Plymouth abounds with motels. Three stand out as family-friendly accommodations.

The **Cold Spring Motel** (188 Court Street; 508–746–2222) is a cheerfully decorated motel near the middle of town, with very reasonable rates.

The **John Carver Inn** (25 Summer Street; 508–746–7100 or 800–274–1620) is a large hotel/motel right in the middle of town, with a pool and a restaurant on the premises.

Pilgrim Sands (150 Warren Avenue/Route 3A; 508–747–0900) is perfectly located if your family wants to spend time at the beach as well as at Plimoth Plantation: It's right on Long Beach, which is practically across the street from the plantation. Call ahead to request an efficiency apartment. There are two pools—one indoor, one outdoor.

If you love to stay in nice old B & Bs, the **Jackson-Russell-Whitfield House** (26 North Street; 508–746–5289) is a lovingly restored, 1782 house that should suit you nicely. It's centrally located but on a quiet street, and the two large rooms (both with fireplaces) convert beautifully into a family suite.

In addition to nearby Duxbury Beach there are two in-town beaches in Plymouth that are well suited to families. **Nelson Street Beach,** off Water Street, just north of Cranberry World, has good swimming, free parking, and a playground. **Stephen's Field Park** is 1 mile south of Plymouth

Nothing like a day at Duxbury Beach.

center, just off Route 3A, at the end of a short dead-end street called Stephen's Lane (heading south of Route 3A, it's the first left after the fire station). It has free parking, a small duck pond, a beach, tennis courts, picnic tables, and a playground.

If one of the kids needs a new pair of shoes, **Little Shoes** (359 Court Street; 508–747–2226) has a good selection.

When you're ready to eat, head for **Wood's Seafood and Fish Market** (at the end of Town Wharf on the right; 508–746–0261) and treat yourselves to a meal of fresh fish or shellfish. While you wait for your order, look at the fresh fish in the adjoining market: The glass-fronted case is low to the ground, so the kids can get a close look. Ask about the blue lobster that the owner caught a few years ago. Open year-round (except January) for lunch and dinner.

If Thai food is one of your family's favorites, visit **Star of Siam** (Route 3A, Manomet; 508–224–3771), an excellent take-out Thai restaurant in the Manomet area of Plymouth, just a few miles south of Long Beach.

Priscilla Beach Theatre (Rocky Hill Road, Manomet; 508–224–4888), the country's oldest summer-stock-performed-in-a-barn playhouse, presents children's shows from June through mid-September on Friday and Saturday at 10:30 A.M. The theater also runs a performing arts day camp (one- and two-week programs). Call ahead for show schedules and for more information about the day camp.

CARVER/SOUTH CARVER

Along Route 58 in Carver (and on many back roads in the area as well), your family may see some of the state's **cranberry bogs.** Half of the country's cranberry crop comes from the marshy, sandy bogs in this area, and cranberries are Massachusetts's number-one agricultural product. When it's harvest time (mid-September through early November), the farmers use machines to literally shake the berries from their vines. They corral the berries into large crimson islands, then use enormous vacuum hoses to scoop the harvest into trucks.

Bike, hike, fish, or swim at **Myles Standish State Forest** (Cranberry Road, South Carver; 508–866–2526), just a twenty-minute drive from Plymouth. The 14,635-acre park was Massachusetts's first state forest when it was created in 1916. There are miles of quiet walking trails, bike paths, fifteen ponds (two, Fearing Pond and College Pond, are designated for swimming; the rest are for fishing), and lots of picnic spots in the forests and meadows. **Camping,** too: The forest has 470 tent/RV sites (no hookups) with rest rooms and hot showers, plus fireplaces and picnic tables at each site. The fee of $6.00 per night includes showers. Take Route 3 to exit 5, turn south on Long Pond Road, and look for the sign to the forest (approximately 2½ miles south).

NEW BEDFORD, DARTMOUTH, AND FALL RIVER

The entire downtown area of New Bedford seems to be a monument to the city's world-famous whaling days, a fitting background for the **New Bedford Whaling Museum** (18 Johnny Cake Hill, New Bedford; 508–997–0046). Kids are justifiably awed by the tools of the trade: enormous hooks, harpoons, and a 90-foot-long whaling bark that kids are welcome to climb on. The scrimshaw collection is remarkable in its quality and depth—among the 2,000 items are a sled and a bird cage carved from whalebone. Do see the twenty-minute silent film of a real whale chase and capture. Open year-round, Monday through Saturday, 9:00 A.M.–5:00 P.M., and Sunday, 1:00–5:00 P.M. (on Sundays in July and August, the museum opens at 11:00 A.M.). From September through June, the whale-chase film is shown on weekends only, at 2:00 P.M.; during July and August the film is shown twice daily, once in the morning and once in the afternoon. Admission is $4.00 for adults, $3.00 for kids six to fourteen, and free for kids under six.

Not far from New Bedford is South Dartmouth and **Demarest Lloyd State Park** (Barney's Joy Road; see directions below), a beautiful beach with calm water, long sandbars, lots of picnic tables in a shady area, and, considering how pleasant this beach is, surprisingly few people. *Directions:* Take Route 93 South to Route 128 North to Route 24 South. Take Route 195 East to the Faunce Corner exit. Turn right onto Faunce Corner Road; cross Route 6 onto Chase Road. At Russell Mills Road turn right; then turn left onto Barneys Joy Neck Road. Follow the signs. From Memorial Day through Labor Day, parking is $5.00 per car.

Just to the west of Dartmouth is Westport, site of another gorgeous beach. **Horseneck State Beach** (Route 88; 508–636–8816) is a 3-mile-long stretch of sand. There's a bathhouse, a snack bar, picnic tables, and good swimming. Watch the kids at low tide, however; the sandbars drop off suddenly. *Directions:* Take Route 93 South to Route 128 North to Route 24 South. Take Route 195 East to Route 88. Follow the signs. From Memorial Day through Labor Day, parking is $5.00 per car.

Though it's inland, Fall River is a major seaport; today **Battleship Cove** (exit 7 off Route 24, Fall River; 508–678–1905) holds six U.S. Navy warships from the World War II era, including a submarine. The USS *Massachusetts* is the biggest, by far, and probably the most interesting to the kids, who will avail themselves of the opportunity to clamber throughout the ship's nine decks (you don't have to take a tour in order to explore the ship). The *Massachusetts* was moved here in 1965 to stand as a permanent memorial to the 13,000 Massachusetts men and women who gave their lives in service during World War II. If your family wants to explore the ship independent of a tour, be sure to pick

KELLY'S TOP ANNUAL EVENTS IN PLYMOUTH AND ON THE SOUTH SHORE

Farm Day at the Children's Museum, June, South Dartmouth; (508) 993–3361

Onset Blues Festival, August, Onset, Buzzards Bay; (508) 295–7072

Plymouth Lobster Festival, August, Plymouth; (508) 746–8500

Fall River Celebrates America Festival, August, Fall River; (508) 676–8226

Feast of the Blessed Sacrament, August, New Bedford; (508) 992–6911

Plimoth Plantation's Thanksgiving Celebration, November, Plymouth; (508) 746–1622

up a brochure when you arrive; it's easy to get lost. Try out the hammocks that served as the sailors' bunks, climb the turrets, and admire the enormous main deck. There's a snack bar, too. Open year-round, daily, 9:00 a.m.–5:00 p.m. Admission is $8.00 for adults, $4.00 for kids six to fourteen, and free for kids under six.

Also at Battleship Cove is the **Fall River Carousel** (508–324–4300), a restored merry-go-round that was moved here from Dartmouth in the early 1990s. The horses are hand-carved and hand-painted. Bring a picnic lunch; there's a nice grassy area next to the carousel. During the summer there are lots of scheduled kid-oriented events here. From Memorial Day through Labor Day, open daily, 10:00 A.M.–10:00 P.M.; after Labor Day to Memorial Day, open Friday through Sunday, 11:00 A.M.–5:00 P.M.; closed January. Rides are 75 cents each.

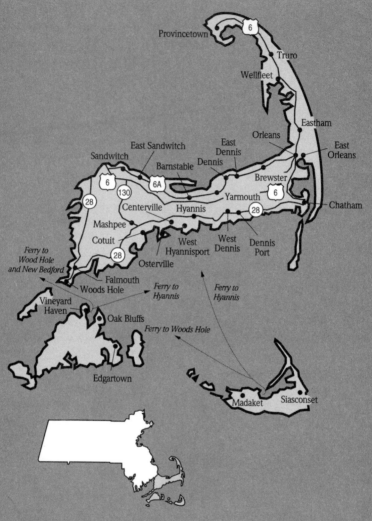

Cape Cod, Martha's Vineyard, and Nantucket

Cape Cod, Martha's Vineyard, and Nantucket

Shaped like a bent arm and stretching 60 miles into the Atlantic, the peninsula of Cape Cod offers nearly 300 miles of beaches, along with acres of nature preserves, dozens of pretty villages, and an abundance of top-notch inns and restaurants that welcome families. At the fist of the Cape's arm, funky Provincetown surrounds the Pilgrim Monument, a replica of the Campanile in Siena. The spectacular view of the curving Cape and the surrounding ocean and bay is worth the climb up the tower's 116 steps. Regardless of the season, visit one or more of the first-class beaches along the Cape's eastern edge. A fun way to keep kids interested during the short drives from town to town is to make the trip into a lighthouse tour. There are seven working lighthouses on the Cape, from Provincetown all the way to Woods Hole.

SANDWICH AND THE CAPE COD CANAL

When you drive over the Sagamore Bridge, you end up on Route 6 in Sandwich. Few visitors stop here; most zip on by on their way to the beaches and cottages of the outer Cape. Sandwich, however, stands out as one of the only Cape towns that you can visit without a car: You can travel to Sandwich by train from Hyannis, tour the village's family-oriented attractions by trolley, and travel back, all in an afternoon.

Although the town of Onset isn't on the Cape, it's relevant to a chapter about the Cape's western end because its Town Pier is the takeoff point for the **Cape Cod Canal Cruises** up and down the calm waters of the 17-mile-long man-made Cape Cod Canal. This is the best way to see the canal. Cruises are available from May through October. Trip times vary from two to four hours. For more information write to Cape Cod Canal Cruises, Box 3, Onset 02558, or call (508) 295–3883.

The well-maintained **Cape Cod Canal Bike Trail** borders the canal on both banks. The trail along the Cape side is less hilly and further removed from auto traffic than the mainland-side trail. Access points along the Cape side of the canal are as follows: in Sandwich, at the U.S. Engineering Station; in Sagamore, from Pleasant Street; from the Bourne Bridge; and at the Buzzards Bay Recreation area next to the Bourne Bridge. Families should avoid crossing either bridge with children, either on foot or on bicycle. If you must cross the canal on your bikes, use the Sagamore Bridge (its sidewalk is safer), and don't ride—walk. The bridges are narrow, motorists tend to exceed the speed limit, and since the bridges' auto lanes are so narrow, drivers aren't looking out for pedestrians or bikers—they're avoiding cars in adjacent lanes.

On a bright day the **Sandwich Glass Museum** (129 Main Street, Town Hall Square, Sandwich; 508–888–0251) is a colorful sight to behold. Since much of the museum's collection is displayed in front of windows, sunlight is very much a part of the installation. Sandwich is internationally known for its glassware, the making of which was most active during the nineteenth century. An excellent video and a diorama explain the glass-making process. April to October, open daily; November to March, open Wednesday through Sunday (except in January, when the museum is closed).

Thousands of dolls of every shape, size, national origin, and whimsical costume are packed into the two-floor **Yesteryears Doll Museum** (Main and River streets, Sandwich; 508–888–1711), situated just down the street from the glass museum. Open mid-May to mid-October, Monday through Saturday, 10:00 A.M.–4:00 P.M. Admission is $3.00 for adults and 50 cents for kids.

The cottage by a duck pond is the **Thornton W. Burgess Museum** (4 Water Street; 508–888–6870), which houses books and memorabilia of

KELLY'S TOP FAMILY ADVENTURES ON CAPE COD, MARTHA'S VINEYARD, AND NANTUCKET

1. Cape Cod National Seashore
2. Nauset Beach, East Orleans
3. Cliffs at Gay Head, Martha's Vineyard
4. Jetties Beach, Nantucket
5. Fisheries Aquarium, Woods Hole
6. Flying Horses Carousel, Martha's Vineyard
7. Whale-watching trips from Provincetown
8. Chatham Fish Pier
9. Provincetown Tower

the renowned author Burgess—he wrote the Mother West Wind stories about the Reddy Fox and Paddy the Beaver characters—as well as animal costumes that kids can try out themselves. The 10:30 A.M. story hour ($1.00 per person) takes place every day in July and August and on most holidays; during the rest of the year, story hour is at 10:30 A.M. on Tuesday, Wednesday, and Saturday. From April to December the museum is open Monday through Saturday, 10:00 A.M.–4:00 P.M., and Sunday, 1:00 P.M.–4:00 P.M.; from January to March it's open Tuesday through Saturday, 10:00 A.M.–4:00 P.M. $1.00 donation is requested.

Adjacent to the Burgess Museum is the **Green Briar Nature Center and Jam Kitchen** (6 Discovery Hill Road, East Sandwich; 508–888–6870). The Nature Center comprises fifty-seven acres of gardens and forests laced with easy walking trails. The Thornton W. Burgess Society runs a full program of nature walks and natural history classes, mostly geared toward kids, throughout the year. After you explore the Nature

Center, stop in at the Jam Kitchen, an old-fashioned kitchen in a pondside building that looks like it's right out of one of Burgess's stories. The Jam Kitchen sells natural jams, jellies, and pickled goods, and they'll show you how to make your own, too. Free.

Heritage Plantation (Grove and Pine streets; 508–888–3300) holds an interesting collection of antique cars in mint condition exhibited in a replica of a round Shaker stone barn (if you want to see the real thing, visit the Hancock Shaker Village near Pittsfield; see the chapter on the Berkshires). Toy-soldier fans enjoy the collection of several thousand hand-painted miniature soldiers. Gardening enthusiasts and kids with lots of energy love to roam the acres of meticulously tended paths that wind through fantastic flower gardens and blooming shrubs. The plantation is open daily from mid-May through October, 10:00 A.M.–5:00 P.M. Admission is $7.00 for adults, $3.50 for kids six to eighteen, and free for kids under five.

The **Glasstown Trolley** makes the circular trip from the railroad station to the Sandwich Glass Museum, Heritage Plantation, and the Dan'l Webster Inn every hour during the summer, 9:00 A.M.–5:00 P.M. All-day fares are $5.00 for adults, $3.00 for kids four to twelve, and free for kids under four.

WEST BARNSTABLE, CENTERVILLE, AND HYANNIS

Barnstable is the Cape's largest town: Its 60 square miles include the villages of Barnstable and West Barnstable along Cape Cod Bay, and Cotuit, Marstons Mills, Osterville, Centerville, and Hyannis along Nantucket Sound. These villages differ greatly. Hyannis is the commercial center of the Cape, as well as its most populated and most crowded town. If you are coming to the Cape to get away from crowds, malls, and traffic, you should avoid Hyannis. If you like the bustle of a busy harbor town, however, you'll enjoy Hyannis— but be sure to get out into the quieter villages that border it on the north and west. By the way, while you're in Hyannis, don't bother looking for Kennedys: When they're at their private compound on the town's western edge, they're on vacation, too, and they keep well out of sight.

A stately church that poses atop a slight hill, the **West Parish Meetinghouse** (corner of Route 149 and Meetinghouse Way, West Barnstable, just north of exit 5 off Route 6; 508–362–4445) is our family's favorite church on the Cape. We don't attend services; rather, we just like to go in when a friendly parishioner is there to let us in to marvel at the big windows, plain pews, and historic atmosphere—it's the second oldest surviving meetinghouse on the Cape.

A good comparison to this oh-so-colonial meetinghouse is only twenty minutes away in the neighboring village of Mashpee. Built in 1684, the **Old Indian Meetinghouse** (Meetinghouse Way near the Route 28 intersection, Mashpee) is the *oldest* surviving meetinghouse on the Cape. Despite the colorful quilts that hang on the walls, this little church manages to be much more solemn than its neighbor in West Barnstable; it's located on the edge of a cemetery that was once for Wampanoag tribe members only (their gravestones are now huddled into a forlorn corner). There is a note of whimsy, however. Tell the kids to climb up the narrow stairs into the choir loft—they'll find the skillful carvings of old ships, masterfully executed by bored parishioners about one hundred years ago. Open June to August: Wednesday, 10:00 A.M.–4:00 P.M.; Friday, 10:00 A.M.–3:00 P.M.; and Sunday for 11:00 A.M. services; open September to May, by appointment only or by chance.

At Barnstable's lovely beach on Cape Cod Bay, the dunes of 6-mile-long **Sandy Neck Beach** (off Route 6A, West Barnstable) protect Barnstable Harbor from heavy surf. They also form one of the Cape's finest barrier beaches, and one that's rarely crowded. There's an adjacent parking lot, rest rooms, changing rooms, and a snack bar. Parking costs $8.00.

On Nantucket Sound, **Centerville Beach** is a busy place that's popular with teenagers as well as families. The water is warmer here than on the north or east coasts of the Cape. Centerville Beach has lots of parking, changing rooms and showers, rest rooms, and a snack bar at the beach (and plenty of clam-shack-type eateries within a few minutes' walk of the beach). Parking costs $8.00.

Within a few minutes' drive or bike ride from Craigville Beach, **Centerville Corners** (1338 Craigville Beach Road; 800–242–1137 or 508–775–7223) is a pleasant motel that's perfect for families who want

The warm waters of Nantucket Sound make a wonderful playground.
(Photo by Peter Simon)

a beach vacation in one of the quieter towns on the Cape's south coast. All rooms are doubles with private bath. Continental breakfast is included in all rates. There is an indoor pool, a large lawn, and croquet and badminton equipment.

Across the street in a converted garage, the venerable **Four Seas** (360 South Main Street, Centerville; 508–775–1394) serves some of the best ice cream on the Cape—and it's all homemade. Many regulars' favorite is peach, one of the many flavors that owner Dick Warren and his clan make from fresh fruit. Lunchbox-type food is served here, too; PB&J, cream cheese and olive, and tuna salad sandwiches make a great appetizer for a main course of ice cream. Open spring and summer only.

If you find yourselves in Hyannis and you'd rather not venture far to go to a beach, wide **Kalmus Park Beach** is a good spot for families. There are gentle waves, fine sand, and a sheltered area for toddlers, as well as rest rooms and a snack bar; parking costs $8.00. **Veterans Park Beach,** just to the north of Kalmus Park, has lots of picnic tables and other facilities; parking costs $8.00. Kalmus Park Beach is at the end of Ocean Street; Veterans Park Beach is parallel to Ocean Street, at the end of Gosnold Street.

A short walk from Kalmus Park and Veterans Park beaches, tree-filled **Captain Gosnold Village** (230 Gosnold Street, Hyannis; 508–775–9111) is a terrific place for families who want to spend a few nights in busy Hyannis. The cottages are the best deal for families here—they're quite large, with TVs and fully equipped kitchens. Also here are a pool, a basketball court, lawn-game equipment, and gas grills. Open May to October.

Another good family-friendly spot in Hyannis, this one in the harbor area, is **Anchor Inn** (1 South Street, Hyannis, 508–775–0357). The only hotel in Hyannis with its own boat-docking facilities, it has a very salty atmosphere and a harborside pool.

One of the highlights of a trip through busy Hyannis is a tour of the **Cape Cod Potato Chip Factory** (Breeds Hill Road, off Route 132, Hyannis; 508–775–7253), followed by lots of free samples. Open weekdays year-round, 10:00 A.M.–4:00 P.M.

The 1¾-hour ride on the **Cape Cod Scenic Railroad,** an old-fashioned train from Hyannis to Sandwich, is fun for kids. Views of the Cape's piney forests and cranberry bogs line the route, and the small village of Sandwich is a nice place to stroll for a couple of hours before you catch the train back to Hyannis. The train leaves from the station at Main and Center streets in downtown Hyannis. Operates May through October, weekends and holidays only; departures at 10:00 A.M. and at 12:30 and 3:00 P.M.

YARMOUTH AND DENNIS

Yarmouth and Dennis cover both the Bay and the Sound coasts of the mid-Cape, as well as the congestion of Route 28 and the peaceful residential areas north of Route 6A and south of Route 28.

A fine beach for families, **Gray's Beach** (off Centre Street from Route 6A, Yarmouth) has another attraction—the long wooden Bass Hole Boardwalk, which stretches over a salt marsh. Kids love to scamper along the elevated walkway; it's also fun to peer out over the marshy grasses and flowers. The beach has calm water, picnic tables, rest rooms, and a playground. Parking is $7.00.

Among the many miniature golf courses that line Route 28 in these two towns, the most inventive is **Pirate's Cove** (782 Main Street, South Yarmouth; 508–394–6200). The course is laid out around a pirate ship that sits in a lagoon-like pond, surrounded by "cliffs" and "waterfalls" that are incorporated into the course.

When you finish minigolfing and you're in the mood for lunch or dinner, head down the road to **the Lobster Boat** (681 Main Street, West Yarmouth, 508–775–0486). The pirate theme and decor are the same here, and you'll have a choice of reasonably priced seafood dishes, as well as hot dogs, fried chicken, and the like.

If you want to stay in the Yarmouth-Dennis area, the **Lighthouse Inn** (1 Lighthouse Road, West Dennis; 508–398–2244) is an affordable, family-oriented resort that's right on Nantucket Sound, near the Bass River. Accommodations consist of rooms and cottages scattered across nine well-maintained acres. On-site attractions and activities include a working lighthouse, tennis courts, a pool, miniature golf, shuffleboard, a private beach, and lots of planned activities for kids.

Not far away is 1-mile-long **West Dennis Beach** (off Davis Beach Road), which borders a flat salt marsh and several tidal streams. It's a busy place in the summer: The eastern end is for Dennis residents only, and the rest of it is taken over by families who park in the enormous parking lot (so big that it rarely fills, unusual for a good Cape beach) and enjoy the beach and its many facilities—good swimming, lots of lifeguard stations, rest rooms, showers, play areas with swing sets, and a snack bar. Parking costs $8.00.

The **Cape Cod Rail Trail** is an 8-foot-wide, 20-mile-long asphalt path that follows the old (discontinued) railroad tracks running from Route 134 in South Dennis to Locust Road in Eastham. To pick up the trail, take exit 9 off Route 6 in Dennis, turn south on Route 134, and travel approximately ¼ mile. The trail ends in Wellfleet, just east of Route 6, near the Wellfleet Chamber of Commerce information booth (where, when the booth is open in the spring and summer, you can pick up maps of local bike routes).

Scargo Tower (off Scargo Hill Road in Dennis) isn't that tall a tower —only 28 feet—but the high hill it sits on makes the tower a great place to take in the terrific view of Cape Cod Bay and the Cape's midsection.

Dennis Port, one of the villages in Dennis, is home to the 4,000-square-foot **Discovery Days Children's Museum** (444 Route 28, Dennis Port; 508–398–1600), which houses a broad variety of interactive educational (but fun) exhibits and organized activities. Mid-June through Labor Day, open daily, 9:30 A.M.–7:30 P.M.; Labor Day through early June, open Wednesday to Monday, 10:00 A.M.–5:00 P.M. Admission is $4.50 for adults and $4.00 for kids.

BREWSTER

Brewster was home to dozens of ship captains during the nineteenth century, many of whom built beautiful homes along what is now Route 6A. Today when the tide is out, Brewster's beaches along the bay—Sea Street Beach, Paines Creek Beach, and Point of Rocks Beach—are a fun spot for kids to explore the miles and miles of sun-warmed tidal pools and skittering seaside animals, birds, and bugs.

If your family would rather not swim in salt water, **Nickerson State Forest** (3488 Route 6A, Brewster; 508–896–3491) is a great place for you —it has several large freshwater ponds. The park also features hiking trails, fishing, bike trails, and camping. Skating and cross-country skiing are popular in the winter. You'll see lots of local families here, by the way.

Brewster is also home to three excellent family-oriented attractions. The **Bassett Wild Animal Farm** (620 Tubman Road, between Routes 124 and 137; 508–896–3224) has a small collection of exotic and domestic animals—lemurs, peacocks, llamas, goats, and more—that appeal mostly to toddlers and young children. The farm is open daily from mid-May to mid-September, 10:00 A.M.–5:00 P.M. Admission is $5.50 for adults and kids over twelve, $3.75 for kids two to twelve.

The six buildings of the **New England Fire and History Museum** (Route 6A, Brewster; 508–896–5711) hold a variety of historic firefighting equipment, a diorama of the Great Chicago Fire, and other exhibits, including a fireboat that kids can climb on. Open Memorial Day to Labor Day, weekdays 10:00 A.M.–4:00 P.M., and weekends noon–4:00 P.M. Admission is $4.50 for adults and $2.50 for kids five to twelve.

Finally, the **Cape Cod Museum of Natural History** (869 Route 6A, Brewster; 508–896–3867) does a terrific job of teaching kids (and their parents) about the Cape's fragile ecology. The museum also runs tours of Monomoy Island Wildlife Refuge (see the description under "Chatham" in this chapter). May through mid-October, it's open daily, 9:30 A.M.–4:30 P.M.; mid-October through May, it's closed Monday. Admission is $4.50 for adults and $2.50 for kids five to twelve.

ORLEANS AND EAST ORLEANS

For families Orleans's main attraction is actually in East Orleans—**Nauset Beach.** Nine miles long and picture-perfect, backed by high dunes, it's one of the Cape's best beaches. If you're willing to walk a bit, Nauset Beach is so long that you will be able to stake out your own territory even on the busiest summer weekends. If you want to stay near the lifeguards, however, stay within the marked area. There's a large bathhouse with rest rooms, changing rooms, and showers; there's also a good snack bar with outdoor picnic tables. The parking lot is large, but parking fees are stiff: on summer weekends it's $10.00 for nonresidents; on weekdays, $8.00. From exit 12 off Route 6, turn right onto Eldredge Park Way, right onto Tonset Road, right onto Main Street, and then left onto Beach Road, which leads straight to Nauset Beach.

Skaket Beach, Orleans's bay beach, is popular with families who enjoy playing in tidal flats. Facilities include rest rooms, changing rooms, and a snack bar. The parking lot isn't large; arrive early. Parking fees are the same as at Nauset Beach, and you can park at both beaches for the same price during one day. Take exit 12 off Route 6, turn right onto Route 6A, turn left onto Main Street, and turn left onto Skaket Beach Road, which ends at the beach.

Land Ho! (corner of Route 6A and Eldredge Park Way; 508–255–5165) is a great place for a bite to eat after an afternoon at the beach. The kale soup is a specialty here, but everything's good. Note the license plates and business signs that show just how local a local hangout this place is. Open daily, year-round.

EASTHAM

Eastham is the place where Myles Standish and his band met their first Native Americans in 1620, after the Pilgrims' first landing in Provincetown and before they found and settled in Plymouth. The meeting spot is commemorated by a bronze marker at the top of the dunes of **First Encounter Beach,** a quiet bay beach in Eastham. From Route 6 turn left on Samoset Road. Parking is $5.00.

Today most visitors go to Eastham to enter the **Cape Cod National Seashore,** which covers nearly 27,000 acres of the outer Cape. It is administered by the National Park Service. Be sure to visit the **Salt Pond Visitors Center** in Eastham, where helpful guides offer complete information on the seashore as well as orientation talks and guided field trips. Please respect the rules set forth by the Park Service; they are in place to protect this unique and fragile area.

Park at **Little Creek Parking Lot** for a free bus trip to **Coast Guard Beach,** one of the best beaches along the National Seashore. The bathhouse is one of the Cape's best. There's a parking lot, too. From Route 6 take Nauset Road, which passes the Salt Pond Visitors Center, and continue on to Doane Road. Little Creek Road will be on the left.

Across the road from the Salt Pond Visitors Center is the **Eastham Historical Society Museum.** Housed in an 1869 schoolhouse building, the museum itself is interesting, though its attractions pale in comparison to the wonders of the National Seashore—but kids enjoy the up-close view of the **whale jawbones** that form the entrance to the museum property.

The red-striped lighthouse called **Nauset Light** has a complicated history. In 1923, the brick building was moved to its current location from Chatham, where it was part of a twin-light setup that was discontinued that year. The site it now occupies is the site of the first of the three light-houses that sat in a row on the cliffs of Nauset from 1838 until 1911. The original "Three Sisters" were moved to Cable Road at Cape Cod National Seashore, not far from the Salt Pond Visitors Center. The National Park Service provides tours of the original brick lighthouses during the summer; ask for a schedule at the Salt Pond Visitors Center information desk. Nauset Light's single red stripe helps mariners to distinguish it from other Cape Cod lighthouses during the day. The round ball at the top of the tower is called a ventilator ball; it allows air to circulate and cool the lantern room, where the lighthouse's beam rotates.

WELLFLEET

The focus in Wellfleet falls equally on the arts and the natural world. Many of the year-rounders and summer-house owners who live in or near Well-fleet's tiny, picturesque harbor are artists, writers, actors, and other arts-oriented people; under their influence several arts day camps are run each summer for children and families.

As is the case in Truro, well over half of Wellfleet's area is conservation land. In this case, much of it is in the care of the Cape Cod National Seashore; the rest is the 750-acre **Wellfleet Bay Wildlife Sanctuary** (west side of Route 6, off West Road; 508–349–2615), which offers myriad nature-oriented activities for families: bird and bat watches, trips through salt marshes, guided trail walks at all hours of the day and night, and several excellent self-guided walking trails where you'll see a variety of birds and coastal animals (watch for turtles). If you know you'll be in the area, and you want to know more about this superb resource for family-oriented activities, write to P.O. Box 238, Wellfleet 02663, for schedules and reservation information. If you've been a member of the Audubon Society for at least a year, you and your family can camp here. From May through October the visitor center is open daily, 9:00 A.M.–5:00 P.M.; from November through April it's open the same hours on Tuesday to Sunday. Trails are open from dawn to dusk year-round. Admission charges are

$3.00 per adult to enter and walk on the trails, $2.00 per child. Excursion costs vary, usually $25–$35 per day.

Of the arts-oriented day camps in Wellfleet, the best is **Artscape** (Coles Neck Road; 508–349–6787), where the artist-teachers help kids use objects that they collect on nature walks—driftwood, sand, and the like—to express their feelings. Morning and full-day programs are available in one-week increments in July and August.

Wellfleet is a cottage colony mecca. One of the best is **Surfside Colony,** on Ocean View Drive along the Cape Cod National Seashore. One-, two-, and three-bedroom cottages are available, all with good kitchens, fireplaces, and screened-in porches; some have roof decks as well. Rates are $600–$1,200 per week. Write to P.O. Box 237, South Wellfleet 02663, or call (508) 349–3959.

The **Wellfleet Drive-In** (on Route 6 just north of the Eastham-Wellfleet line; 508–349–7176) wears two hats: From 8:00 A.M. to 4:00 P.M. on Monday, Wednesday, Thursday, weekends, and holidays throughout the summer, it's a flea market, and in the evenings it's a real drive-in movie theater, with a playground and a snack bar.

If you need some early morning sustenance before you head to the beach, try the **Lighthouse** (Main Street; 508–349–3681). They serve all three meals, but their hearty breakfasts are particularly good.

The **Bayside Lobster Hutt** (Commercial Street, Wellfleet; 508–349–6333) is a noisy, casual restaurant that most of Wellfleet's summer visitors recommend to day-trippers as the best place to eat after a day at the beach. Seating is family-style at long tables; predictably, the menu leans heavily toward seafood, including Wellfleet's famous oysters. There's take-out, too.

Smaller, quieter **Painter's Lunch** (15 Kendrick Avenue; 508–349–7343) also has good seafood, as well as creative linguica dishes.

If you're looking for freshwater swimming, try **Long Pond** (off East Main Street; take Long Pond Road), where you'll find a shady picnic area and a float in the middle of the pond. Ocean beaches include **Marconi Beach** (part of the Cape Cod National Seashore; $5.00 parking fee), which has a great bathhouse, and **Cahoon Hollow,** and **White Crest beaches,** both town beaches. White Crest is broader and has a larger parking lot ($10 parking fee for both; rest rooms here, too).

TRURO

Truro is best known for its beaches and the plethora of summer houses and cottages that dot its high hills and dunes. For such a beautiful place, it's remarkably untouristy. To reach the town center, as it were, of Truro, take the Pamet Road exit off Route 6.

The **Pilgrim Heights** area of the National Seashore, in North Truro, has a nice walk to the place where the Cape's first European visitors found their first fresh water. Take the **Pilgrim Spring Walk** from the interpretive shelter off Route 6. The part of **Head of the Meadow Beach** that's maintained by the Cape Cod National Seashore has a beach house with rest rooms. There are no lifeguards here, but on a calm day this beach is one of the best along the National Seashore. From Route 6 turn right onto Head of the Meadow Road. Parking costs $5.00.

The first light that sailors see when they make the trip from Europe to Boston is that of **Cape Cod Light,** the oldest lighthouse on the Cape. Because it was built on the highlands of Truro, it is also known as **Highland Light.** The present buildings date from 1857, but the first lighthouse constructed on this spot went up in 1798. Highland Light's precarious position on eroded cliffs makes it likely that it will tumble into the ocean unless the Truro Historical Society's efforts can save it. At night children enjoy looking for the light's bright white beam, which is visible during the drive on Route 6 from Truro to Provincetown. Highland is the highest (182 feet above sea level) as well as the tallest (66 feet) lighthouse on the Cape; it's also one of the Cape's two manned lighthouses (the other is Nobska Light, in Woods Hole).

Bayside **Corn Hill Beach** is the place where Miles Standish and his desperately hungry group "borrowed" their first corn from the natives. A marker on the cliff at the edge of the bay indicates the spot where the event took place. This is also a great place for shelling. Take Castle Road from the center of Truro (follow signs from Route 6) and follow it to Corn Hill Beach. Parking costs $5.00. *Note:* No lifeguards here.

PROVINCETOWN

At the fist end of the Cape, Provincetown is a funky collection of open-minded artists, fishermen, windworn buildings, and seaside moors. Go here for the beaches, the whale watching, and the people-watching, which is especially good in this, New England's most tolerant seaside community.

When it was built in 1827, **Long Point** was the center of a busy fishing community on the tip of the Cape. Now isolated at the end of a long breakwater, Long Point Lighthouse (and its companion, Wood End) can best be viewed from the rotary at the end of Commercial Street (while you're here, look for the plaque that commemorates the first landing place of the Pilgrims). If your family is up for a long walk along a rocky breakwater (not appropriate for young children or for anyone without sturdy footwear and good balance), park the car at the rotary and walk along the breakwater for about half an hour to reach Long Point.

About another half-hour's walk farther, at the end of the breakwater, **Wood End Lighthouse** is unusual in that it is a square white tower; most lighthouses are circular. Wood End was built in 1873. It flashes a red light every fifteen seconds, whereas Long Point flashes a green light; together they mark Provincetown Harbor's entrance.

Pilgrim Lake Sand Dunes in the **Province Lands** area of Cape Cod National Seashore is the only place along the National Seashore where visitors can legally walk over the enormous sand dunes that roll across this part of the Cape. Previous visitors have worn away much of the sand and, with it, the beach grass that covers and preserves the dunes; therefore, the National Park Service restricts foot traffic on the dunes to this area. While you're in the Province Lands area, stop at the **Province Lands Visitors Center**; it's open 9:00 A.M.–6:00 P.M. during the summer and 9:00 A.M.–4:30 P.M. during the spring and fall.

Race Point and **Herring Cove Beaches** are Provincetown's best beaches for families. A snack bar and gentler waves are at bayside Herring Cove, whereas large sand dunes and fewer crowds are at Race Point; showers and rest rooms are at both. Race Point is at the end of Race Point Road, off Route 6; Herring Cove Beach is at the end of Route 6. In either case, arrive at these beaches before 11:00 A.M. during the summer to be sure of a parking place ($5.00).

The 2-mile walk to reach **Race Point Lighthouse** is along Race Point Beach (bring refreshments, especially drinks; the long sandy walk back to the car can be tough for kids). Race Point Lighthouse was established in

1816 to help ships navigate from the ocean around the treacherous "knuckles" of the Cape to Provincetown. Between 1816 and 1946 more than a hundred shipwrecks were recorded in this area. Race Point Lighthouse has a white light and a foghorn that warns ships of low-visibility conditions. If your family doesn't have the energy to take the long walk to Race Point, the best view is from the Province Lands Visitors Center's observation deck. Race Point Lighthouse is also visible from Herring Cove Beach.

You'll see **whale-watching trips** advertised everywhere along the Cape (and in Boston and on the North Shore too, for that matter), but the only good place from which to take one is Provincetown. Why? Because it's closest to Stellwagen Bank, the whales' feeding ground, which is only 6 miles from Provincetown; other trips take much longer to reach the same spot. Most of the whale-watching expeditions from Provincetown are about three and a half hours long, but some last all day. Regardless of the weather on shore, be *sure* to bring a warm sweater and long pants for everyone in your party—even at the height of summer, the wind on the open ocean can be downright cold. The best of the many whale-watch boats is the ***Ranger V,*** which operates from MacMillan Wharf from mid-May to mid-November. Prices range from $10–$18; kids under seven ride free. The ticket office is at the corner of Bradford and Standish streets. For more information call (800) 992–9333 or (508) 487–3322.

The **Provincetown Heritage Museum and Tower** (corner of Center and Commercial streets; 508–487–0666) is worth the visit for the view from the 162-foot-high tower that was modeled after the Campanile in Siena, Italy. On a clear day the view of the curving Cape is breathtaking. In July, August, and September, the museum and tower is open daily, 9:00 A.M.–9:00 P.M.; in April, May, June, October, and November, the tower is open daily, 9:00 A.M.–5:00 P.M.; and from December through March, hours are daily, 9:00 A.M.–4:00 P.M. Admission is $3.00 for everyone over twelve.

Provincetown abounds with restaurants; you shouldn't have trouble finding a place that appeals to your family. Here are a couple of suggestions. **Fat Jack's** (295 Commercial Street; 508–487–4822) is a good bet;

it's a classic burger joint with a nice clientele and a friendly staff. For seafood-loving families, the **Dancing Lobster,** right on MacMillan Wharf (508–487–0900) is a prime place to devour lobsters and other seafood.

There are lots of funky shops along Provincetown's Commercial Street, but a family favorite is **Norma Glamp's Rubber Stamps** (357 Commercial Street; 508–487–1870), which carries the broadest variety of stamps and colorful ink pads you'll ever see. It's a fun spot to pick an unusual souvenir of your family's trip to this unique town.

CHATHAM

Chatham is a village of shingled cottages, with a delightful Main Street full of shops and cafes, and a variety of top-level summer accommodations for families. There are several attractions that are in the don't-miss category for families: the Fish Pier, Chatham Lighthouse, the Friday-evening band concerts at Kate Gould Park, and the Railroad Museum.

Watch the day's catch being unloaded from the observation deck at **Chatham Fish Pier** between 2:00 and 4:00 P.M. It's just north of town, on the corner of Bar Cliff Avenue and Shore Road.

On Main Street between Shore Road and Bridge Street, Chatham Light sits across from a small parking lot, several sets of coin-operated binoculars, and a breathtaking view of the **Chatham Break.** The Break occurred during a ferocious winter storm in 1987, when storm-pounded waves broke through the barrier beach that stretches south from Nauset Beach, forming a separate island (now called South Beach)—and a break in the barrier that had protected Chatham's harbor and coastline from the full brunt of the Atlantic. The break is a spectacular example of the power of weather, wind, and the ocean.

The present building at **Chatham Light** is one of a pair that was built in 1877 (the light's twin building was moved to Nauset in 1923). Chatham's original lighthouses were built in 1808. Heavy erosion, which is still a problem in Chatham, forced the Coast Guard to move the lights back from the coast to the spot where the light stands today. Chatham Light flashes four times every thirty seconds.

The restored depot building of the **Chatham Railroad Museum** (Depot Road; no phone), with its Cheerio-like architectural details, holds an impressive collection of thousands of model trains. Thomas the Tank Engine fans will enjoy the old caboose, which is most kids' favorite object. Open mid-June through mid-September, Tuesday through Saturday, 10:00 A.M.–4:00 P.M. Free admission; donations accepted. There's a great **playground** on Depot Road behind the elementary school, just down the road from the Railroad Museum. The playground has equipment for disabled kids and a separate area for toddlers.

One of the true adventures left for Cape visitors is a trip to **Monomoy Island Wildlife Refuge,** a 2,700-acre wilderness area on two islands that serve as a resting area for migratory birds and a home for as many as 285 species of seaside birds. If your family would like to tour Monomoy, you'll need to arrange a guided tour with one of two organizations: either the Cape Cod Museum of Natural History (call 508–896–3867 for information and reservations) or the Wellfleet Bay Wildlife Sanctuary (508–349–2615). On your tour of the islands (North and South Monomoy), you'll see acres of true seaside wilderness: There are no roads, no buildings, and no electricity. If you don't have time for a guided tour, visit the **Morris Island Visitor Center** (508–945–0594). They don't provide tours, but the helpful staff will provide you with plenty of literature and will point you and the kids toward the ¾-mile self-guided interpretive tour around Morris Island. No dogs, please. *Directions to Morris Island:* From Main Street in Chatham, between Bridge Street and Shore Road, take the first left after Chatham Light. Take the first right; follow Morris Island Road to the visitor center.

One of the nicest motels on Cape Cod is **Pleasant Bay Village** (Route 28, Chatham; mailing address Box 772, Chatham 02633; 800–547–1011 or 508–945–1133). It's a large complex of buildings set on grounds that are so beautifully planted and maintained, it's like a motel in a garden. The kitchens in the efficiency units are well equipped and scrupulously clean. There's a heated pool on the grounds and plenty of room for kids to run around; the facility is also near several nice beaches. *A tip:* The road between Chatham and Orleans can be busy; take the time to drive the kids to the beach rather than allowing them to walk.

If you are going to splurge on a resort-type vacation on the Cape, the **Chatham Bars Inn** (Shore Road, Chatham; 800–527–4884 or 508–

945–0096) is the place to do it. Grand is not an exaggerated description for this place, which offers all the luxuries of a hotel and all the fun of the oceanside. You can select from suites, cottages, and rooms with balconies; there are 152 rooms in all on the twenty-acre property. The inn has a private beach just across Shore Road, with beach chairs, umbrellas, lifeguards, and planned activities, including all-day children's programs. Meals are served in spacious, elegant dining rooms; clam bakes take place on the beach once a week. Open year-round. Room rates are $120–$375, depending on the room and the meal plan you choose.

Another option for beach-loving families is a cottage rental on the nicest private beach in Chatham. The **Horne family** has a variety of cottages, all clean and beautifully maintained. Cottages range from two bedrooms (four persons) for $900 per week to four bedrooms (eight persons) for $1,650 per week. In the off-season (before June 25 and after September 10), three-person families can stay for $585 per week ($25 per additional person). Cottages are located off Morris Island Road (mailing address is P.O. Box 174, Chatham 02633); 508–945–0734.

Go to the **Break-Away Café** (207 Main Street, Chatham; 508–945–5300) for breakfast and lunch just down the road from Chatham Light —yummy pies, muffins, and sandwiches. Open mid-March to November.

Every Friday night from early July through early September, there's a **band concert** at the bandstand in Kate Gould Park on Main Street. Thousands of visitors and locals show up for these evenings to dance to old standards, Sousa marches, and the like.

The best easy-to-reach family beach in Chatham is **Hardings Beach.** It's a long beach with small dunes, restrooms, a snack bar, and a large parking lot (though since it's popular with families, it can fill up before noon in the summer). Parking is $7.00 per day and $35.00 per week.

If you're looking for a deserted beach, take a five-minute water-taxi shuttle ride (call Harbor Marine on Morris Island Road; 508–945–3030) to **South Beach,** which is the part of Nauset Beach that was separated from the mainland by the Chatham Break. Keep in mind that there are no lifeguards and no facilities here; pack a lunch and plenty of water. You'll share the beach with lots of shorebirds, the overflow from Monomoy Island.

FALMOUTH AND WOODS HOLE

West of the large town of Barnstable is Falmouth, a pleasant New England village that pulses with visitors throughout the summer. Its Nantucket Sound coast is lined with guest houses, hotels, and summer homes. The downtown area has some good shopping and a few ice cream parlors, but the main attraction of Falmouth is its coastline: The beaches are terrific, and the many inlets that cut into its coast provide lots of space for private boat mooring.

Of the four beaches that are open to nonresidents, the best are South Cape Beach, Surf Drive Beach, and Old Silver Beach.

South Cape Beach is part of a state park (South Cape Beach State Park) that has several nice nature trails. The beach is the attraction here, though: It's a 2-mile-long barrier beach with a bathhouse, a snack shop, and a big parking lot ($5.00 fee) that rarely fills.

Surf Drive Beach is off Main and Shore streets, on Vineyard Sound. It's popular with sailboarders and sea kayakers, some of whom have beachside "garages" for their boats and gear. It's west of the main part of Falmouth, which keeps much of the summer crowd away. Parking costs $5.00.

Long, sandy **Old Silver Beach** is a great secret: though it's popular with locals and canny sailboarders, few tourists come here. There are warm tidal pools, a bathhouse, and a snack bar. Since it faces west, the sunsets are terrific. It's off Route 28A and Quaker Road in North Falmouth (just north of Woods Hole). Parking costs $10.

The **Cape Cod Children's Museum** (Falmouth Mall on Route 28; 508–457–4667) is a good place to spend a rainy day. It has a bubble room and a pirate ship, both especially popular with the toddler crowd, and the story hours (Tuesday and Friday) and craft workshops are fun for everyone. Admission is $3.00 for anyone over five and $2.00 for kids ages one through four; on Fridays from 5:00 to 8:00 P.M., admission is $1.00.

In late July bring the kids to the **Barnstable County Fair** (Barnstable County Fairgrounds, Route 151, East Falmouth; 508–563–3200) for a dose of old-time fair atmosphere. You'll see livestock shows, oxen pulls, baking contests, a midway, and lots of gooey foods. If you're in the Falmouth-Woods Hole area in the middle of August, you might enjoy cheering on the runners in the **Falmouth Road Race,** an annual 7-mile-race that attracts runners from all over New England (for more information call 508–540–7000).

If your family is in the mood for a pleasant boat ride, an alternative to the Steamship Authority ferry trips to and from Martha's Vineyard is the *Island Queen* (Falmouth Heights Road, Falmouth; 508–548–4800), which departs from its own dock in Falmouth's Inner Harbor. Park the car at the *Island Queen* parking lot on Falmouth Heights Road and take the ferry over to the Vineyard for the day; it's less expensive, and the boat is smaller and more comfortable than the more workmanlike Steamship Authority boats. The *Island Queen* operates May to October.

Not far from the *Island Queen* dock, **Pat's Pushcart** (339 Main Street, East Falmouth; 508–548–5090) serves some of the best unfussy Italian food to be had on the Cape. The staff is fun and friendly, and kids are welcome.

The tiny village of Woods Hole, part of Falmouth, is a fun place for kids to enjoy the Fisheries Aquarium and watch the boats going in and out of tiny Eel Pond, which serves as a harbor and a town center, of sorts. Walk around the pond to see the town's sites: the aquarium, St. Mary's Bell Tower and Garden, the harbor, and the drawbridge. Many families see little more of Woods Hole, however, than the Steamship Authority parking lots and waiting area. This is the place to catch the car ferry to Martha's Vineyard.

The **Shining Sea Bike Path** is a 3⅓-mile trail between Falmouth and Woods Hole that's named for the last line of Falmouth native Katherine Lee Bates's beloved song, "America the Beautiful." The path can be crowded in the summer, and it's hilly in a few spots. Pick it up on Palmer Avenue in Falmouth. From here it winds through forests, goes past Nobska Lighthouse, and ends at Woods Hole Harbor. Park in Hyannis rather than in tiny Woods Hole, which is usually packed to the brim; the **Whoosh** trolley operates between Falmouth and Woods Hole from late May to mid-October (50¢ per passenger).

Nobska Light sits on a bluff above winding Nobska Road between Woods Hole and Falmouth, overlooking Martha's Vineyard, Vineyard Sound, and the Elizabeth Islands. The lighthouse building that stands on this site today was built in 1876. Flashing every six seconds, Nobska's fixed-beacon light provides precise information to mariners: Seen head-on, the beam is white, indicating the safest route into Woods Hole Harbor; seen from either side, the red beam warns mariners against routes that could force them to go aground against the shoals. The light guides thousands of ships each year through the treacherous waters that lead to Woods Hole.

Woods Hole is home to the Woods Hole Oceanographic Institute (WHOI), a research facility that isn't open to the public. Nonetheless, the **National Marine Fisheries Service Aquarium** (Albatross Street, Woods Hole; 508–548–7684) benefits from WHOI's presence; it preserves living sea creatures that are native to the Cape's waters. The touch tanks are low to the ground so that even small toddlers can reach in and feel the crabs, lobsters, turtles, and other forms of sea life. There are microscopes to view tinier sea creatures, as well as tanks with larger fish. The whole place is child-oriented, and the helpful aquarium staff love to hear kids' questions. June to September, it's open daily; October to May, it's open weekdays.

If you want to visit Martha's Vineyard without a car, park in one of the **Steamship Authority**'s parking lots and take the free shuttle bus to the harbor. You don't need a reservation if you're traveling without a car; simply purchase tickets for each person. The trip takes approximately forty-five minutes. During the summer there are as many as fourteen round-trips each day. When we make our annual pilgrimage to the Vineyard, as soon as we've parked the car in line to get on the ferry, one person stays in the car and the others rush over to **Pie in the Sky** (10 Water Street, Woods Hole; 508–540–5475) for muffins, juice, coffee, and sandwiches; it's open year-round.

Woods Hole Passage (186 Woods Hole Road, Woods Hole; 508–548–9575) is a quiet B & B in the northern part of Woods Hole. Rooms are spacious and comfortable, and the enormous backyard is perfect for romping kids. Breakfasts are large and delicious. Open year-round. Rates mid-June through late September are $85–$95, double occupancy, $20 per extra person; off-season, $65–$75.

Spohr's Garden is a privately owned, three-acre garden that's a lovely spot for a walk along grassy paths that are bordered by flower beds, rhododendron, and other flowering bushes. Geese and ducks wander freely, so please leave the dog in the car. The garden is on Fells Road off Oyster Pond Road and is open year-round.

THE ISLANDS: MARTHA'S VINEYARD AND NANTUCKET

The islands of Martha's Vineyard and Nantucket provide more spectacular beaches and seaside atmosphere with less stress and fewer visitors than you'll see on the Cape. The unique character of each island has much to do with their distance from the mainland—at its closest point the Vineyard is only 7 miles from Falmouth, whereas Nantucket is a good 30 miles out to sea. The Vineyard is more populous and cosmopolitan; Nantucket is more traditional and much less crowded, even during the summer. Fertile Martha's Vineyard boasts large expanses of deep forest and acres of rolling farmland, whereas moors cover a large percentage of Nantucket. Nantucket's bike paths and long beaches make for wonderful family vacations; the colorful cottages and Flying Horses Carousel in Oak Bluffs, on the Vineyard, are beloved to the lucky children who live on the island as well as those who visit. Annual visitors treat their island vacations as sacred family rituals, booking their reservations as far as six or eight months ahead; try to make your family's ferry and accommodations plans as early as possible.

MARTHA'S VINEYARD

The 4,400 acres of **Manuel Correllus State Forest** (off Edgartown-West Tisbury Road and Barnes Road; 508–693–2540; open year-round) are crisscrossed with bike trails and hiking trails. Park near the Barnes Road entrance to the park. A preserve that's affiliated with the Audubon Society, **Felix Neck Wildlife Sanctuary** (off Edgartown–Vineyard Haven Road, Edgartown; 508–627–4850; open year-round) comprises 350 acres of forests, marshes, and meadows, as well as beaches and an excellent interpretive center that conducts guided nature walks year-round. There's a pleasant 1½-mile **hiking trail** that leaves from the sanctuary's exhibit building. The visitor center is open daily from June to October, and Tuesday through Sunday from November to May.

A 10-mile flat **bike path** shuttles cyclists between Edgartown and Oak Bluffs. The far end of the Edgartown part of the path leads to Katama and South Beach.

Kids will be more interested in the story of the Liberty Pole than the **Old Schoolhouse Museum** (110 Main Street, Vineyard Haven; 508–693–3860), which, along with being the site of a historic flagpole, holds artifacts of the lives of the earliest European settlers on the Vineyard. During the Revolutionary War British sailors attempted to steal the pole from Vineyard Haven to replace a broken mast. Three little girls got wind of their plot and blew up the pole. Today a replica holds its place. Open mid-June to mid-September, 10:00 A.M. to 2:00 P.M. on weekdays.

An unusual attraction in an unusual town, **Butterflies in Flight** (Circuit Avenue Extension, Oak Bluffs; 508–693–4006) is a large, tentlike structure on the edge of Oak Bluffs Marina that contains thousands of flitting butterflies. On a sunny day you can see them through the canvas, but you should definitely bring the kids inside to see this impressive sight. Open daily mid-May to mid-September.

An old wooden building houses the **Flying Horses** (Circuit Avenue, Oak Bluffs; 508–693–9481), a National Historic Landmark that's wonderfully alive with merry-go-round lovers of all ages (we know lots of childless adults who ride the Flying Horses every summer). It's the oldest operating carousel in the country; the horses were carved in 1876. There's even a brass ring. The colorful cottages of the **Wesleyan Grove Campground** were built during the late nineteenth century to replace the tents used by Methodist parishioners who camped and worshiped here every summer. Please observe the no-bicycles rule and Quiet Time, which begins at dusk and ends at sunrise. The carousel is open daily, mid-April to mid-October. Admission is $1.00 per person.

Giordano's (107 Circuit Avenue, Oak Bluffs; 508–693–0184); serves up enormous portions of spaghetti, fried clams, fried chicken, and the like to the families who flock here. It's open for lunch and dinner, May to mid-September.

Mad Martha's has great homemade ice cream in a fun atmosphere at 117 Circuit Avenue; also at 8 Union Street and 52 Main Street in Vineyard Haven and on North Water Street in Edgartown.

At Moshup Beach on Martha's Vineyard, you can really bury yourself in your work.

A cupola-topped, three-story pink building at the "top" of Circuit Avenue, the **Oak Bluffs Inn** (Circuit Avenue, Oak Bluffs; 800–955–6235 or 508–693–7171) has nine comfortable rooms. Open April to mid-October. Rates run $75–$100.

Bring the kids in to see the funky stuff that's for sale at **Take It Easy, Baby** (142 Circuit Avenue, Oak Bluffs; 508–693–2864): ancient and new jeans and leather jackets, kid-size Doc Martens, old-fashioned nightgowns, hats, and long johns. Open year-round.

The section of Joseph Sylvia State Beach known as **Bend-in-the-Road Beach** is a nice spot for families with kids; no facilities, though there are lifeguards.

Also known as Katama Beach, **South Beach** (off Katama Road, south of Edgartown) is the most popular beach on the island. There are lifeguards, though not all the way along the beach; no facilities. It's not appropriate for small children or weak swimmers, since the undertow can be treacherous. It's also accessible by shuttle bus from Edgartown.

Walk to **Edgartown Lighthouse** from North Water Street. In 1828 the lighthouse was built on what was then a tiny island in Edgartown Harbor; after a storm in the early twentieth century, a sandbar emerged from the water and attached the smaller island to the Vineyard.

For kids the most interesting item at Edgartown's **Vineyard Museum** (8 Cooke Street, Edgartown; 508–627–4441) is the original Fresnel lens from the Gay Head Lighthouse, which is lighted for a few hours every night. From July through Labor Day, the museum is open daily, 10:00 A.M.–4:30 P.M.; from Labor Day to July, it's open Wednesday through Friday afternoons, and Saturday, 10:00 A.M.–4:00 P.M.

Here's a find: In expensive, exclusive Edgartown, you can actually sit down, outdoors, at a cafe-type restaurant called **Among the Flowers** (North Water Street, Edgartown; 508–627–3747) and order a—peanut butter sandwich. Other plain fare is available, too. Open April through June and September through mid-November for breakfast and lunch, and in July and August for breakfast, lunch, and dinner.

A comfortable home in a quiet part of Edgartown, **Summer House** (96 South Summer Street, Edgartown; 508–627–4857) is a B & B that has two large bedrooms and an enormous walled-in backyard. It's run by a schoolteacher who's one of the friendliest Vineyarders we've met. Open mid-May to mid-September. Rates run $110–$150.

Our daughter's trip to the Vineyard isn't complete without a stop to feed the swans and ducks who swim in the lovely little **pond** next to the West Tisbury Police Station.

Below the colorful clay cliffs, **Gay Head Beach** is very popular during the summer. Since parking is limited, and the beach extends south for several miles, it's rarely crowded. This is our family's favorite beach in New England. *Note:* There are no lifeguards here, and the closest rest rooms are on top of the cliffs near the clam shacks. You'll probably see other people climbing up the cliffs; resist the temptation. The worst of the cliffs' erosion is a direct result of foot traffic on the fragile clay. Moreover, the cliffs are the private property of the Wampanoag tribe, who run the town of Gay Head.

Gay Head Lighthouse is a red-brick lighthouse in a spectacular setting; on Friday and Saturday evenings during the summer, you can go up to the lighthouse's observation deck to look out over the cliffs at the sun setting over the Sound.

Visit the llamas at **Takemmy Farm** (State Road, West Tisbury; 508–693–2486). Kids are welcome to pet the strange-looking, large-eyed animals that graze on this small farm, which also features donkeys and an enormous chicken coop. There's a terrific little play area here, too, with swings, slides, and a sandbox. Open Wednesday and Saturday afternoons, year-round.

If you saw the film *Jaws,* you may recognize tiny **Menemsha** and **Dutcher's Dock,** which served as a backdrop in many of the film's harbor shots. It's fun to walk along the dock and watch the fishing folk go about their work. At Beetlebung Corner take Menemsha Cross Road to its end, park, and walk down to the dock.

If you're in Menemsha at dinnertime, your family will certainly enjoy a take-out meal from **Home Port** (North Road, Menemsha; 508–645–2679), a casual seafood restaurant that's just steps from the water. If you want to sit down at Home Port, call ahead; reservations are required. Open mid-May to mid-October.

The location, not the food, is the great thing about the **Aquinnah** (on the cliffs, Gay Head; 508–645–9654), but you won't mind the lackadaisical air of the kitchen, since you'll be busy watching the seagulls and gazing at the view. Open mid-May through June and September through October for breakfast and lunch; open June through August for breakfast, lunch, and dinner.

Surrounded by waving grass and romantic moors, **Duck Inn** (off State Road, Gay Head; 508–645–9018) is a very comfortable, health-oriented B & B that's perfect for stressed-out families. The kids will enjoy Oralee, the inn mascot, a Vietnamese potbellied pig; parents will love the hot tub and massages; and everyone will love the delicious meals. Open year-round. Rates are $75–$135.

NANTUCKET

Nantucket's stocky **Brant Point Lighthouse** is one of New England's shortest lighthouses (it's just 31 feet tall); it's also one of Massachusetts's most photographed spots. Approach it from Easton Street. When you leave

KELLY'S TOP ANNUAL EVENTS ON CAPE COD, MARTHA'S VINEYARD, AND NANTUCKET

Daffodil Festival, April, Nantucket; (508) 228–1700

Rhododendron Festival, Mid-May to Mid-June, Heritage Plantation, Sandwich; (508) 888–3300

Cape Cod Chowder Festival, late June, Cape Cod Melody Tent, Hyannis; (508) 775–6800

West Tisbury Farmer's Market, June through September, West Tisbury, Martha's Vineyard

Fourth of July Fireworks, July 4, Hyannis, Falmouth Heights, Provincetown and Chatham

Mashpee Pow-Wow, July, Heritage Ballfield, Mashpee; (508) 477–0208

Edgartown Regatta, July, and August, Edgartown, Martha's Vineyard

Story Hour at the Atheneum, July and August, Nantucket

Barnstable County Fair, July, Barnstable County Fairgrounds, East Falmouth; (508) 563–3200

Falmouth Road Race, August, Falmouth to Woods Hole; (508) 540–7000

Peter Rabbit's Annual Fair, August, Henry T. Wing School, Sandwich; (508) 888–6870

Illumination Night, Mid-August, Oak Bluffs, Martha's Vineyard

Cape Cod Air Show, Otis Air Force Base, Bourne; (508) 968–4003

Sandcastle and Sculpture Contest, Mid-August, Nantucket; (508) 228–1700

Striped Bass and Bluefish Derby, mid-September through mid-October, Martha's Vineyard

Tivoli Day and Pro-Am Bike Race, a Sunday in mid-September, Oak Bluffs, Martha's Vineyard
Christmas Stroll, first Saturday in December, Nantucket

the island by ferry, you'll see lots of people throwing pennies overboard as the ship rounds the Brant Point. This tradition supposedly ensures that a Nantucket visitor will return to the island.

Visit the excellent **Whaling Museum** (Broad Street; 508–228–1736) to see a vivid explanation of the phrase "Nantucket sleigh ride." That's what happens when your harpoon gets stuck in a whale's back and the whale decides to take you and your companions for a ride through the waves. Open year-round. Admission is $8.00 for adults and $5.00 for kids.

Maria Mitchell was the first woman to discover a comet, and she did it on Nantucket, from an observatory that her father constructed on top of his bank building on Main Street in Nantucket. She was the librarian at the Nantucket Atheneum for twenty years before becoming an astronomy professor at Vassar College (another first—first female astronomy professor). The library of the **Maria Mitchell Center** (2 Vestal Street; 508–228–9219) has a section for kids, as well as a fascinating collection of Maria's nineteenth-century science books and papers. Next door is Maria's birthplace, which holds the telescope she was using when she discovered "her" comet. The Mitchell home is topped by the only roof walk on the island that's open to the public. Admission is $5.00 and $2.00 for kids; library is free.

Jetties Beach is off Bathing Beach Road from North Beach Road. Lots of facilities—rest rooms, showers, a snack bar, a playground, rental boats, and rental chairs—make it Nantucket's best beach for families. This is where the annual Sandcastle and Sculpture Day contest is held in mid-August.

Children's Beach, off South Beach Street, is appropriately named because it's perfect for very small children. It offers a bathhouse, an excellent snack bar, a playground, a grassy play area, a horseshoe pit, picnic tables, and organized activities for kids on Friday and weekends. Sunday-evening band concerts are held in July and August.

Surfside's heavy surf makes it inappropriate for families with small children, but strong swimmers who love bodysurfing will find heaven here. This long beach can be crowded with college kids and surf casters, but Surfside is long enough to accommodate everyone. Facilities include a large parking lot, rest rooms, showers, and a snack bar.

The White Elephant and the **Breakers** (Easton Street; mailing address, P.O. Box 359; 800–475–2637 or 508–228–2500) is an elegant resort that best accommodates families during its "Kids Only" program in the summer months, when activities are provided for the kids from early morning into the evening hours. The cottages are the best family deal here—they have kitchens and spacious living rooms. Open late May to mid-October.

The Beachside (30 North Beach Street; 800–322–4433 or 508–228–2241) is a double-decker motel near Jetties Beach; a few two-room suites are available. Open mid-April to mid-October. Children under eight stay free in their parents' room.

Nesbitt Inn (21 Broad Street; mailing address, P.O. Box 1019; 508–228–0156 or 228–2446) is a pleasant inn that welcomes families who don't mind sharing bathrooms with other guests. There's a swingset in the backyard and games in the living room; families are welcome to use the grill in the backyard. Breakfast is provided. Open year-round.

The early hours are for families at the **Atlantic Café** (15 South Water Street; 508–228–0570), a relaxing, reasonably priced restaurant that serves excellent chowder and a kid's menu. *Note:* The place gets noisy later in the evening when the bar area fills with the college crowd. Open year-round.

'Sconset Beach is a long, narrow beach that can be seaweedy, but your family may overlook the inconvenience if you enjoy having lots of room to yourselves. There's a playground here, too. Families enjoy biking to 'Sconset Beach via the 7-mile **'Sconset Bike Path,** which parallels

Milestone Road. There are some mild hills. It's approximately one hour to 'Sconset. The **Surfside Bike Path** is a 3-mile-long, flat trail that leads from the town of Nantucket to its best beach. Take Main Street to Pleasant Street; turn right onto Atlantic Avenue and proceed to Surfside. The path can be crowded.

CAPE COD BASEBALL LEAGUE

Looking for something to fill your family's summer vacation evenings? Between mid-June and early September, the **Cape Cod Baseball League** is just the thing. Ten towns on the Cape field teams made up of the country's top college baseball players, who play before enthusiastic small crowds and, more often than not, big-league scouts who discovered the likes of Carlton Fisk and Will Clark, among others, on the Cape's diamonds. Players conduct weekly clinics for kids, too. If you're planning ahead, write to Box 164, South Harwich 02661 (508–362–3036).

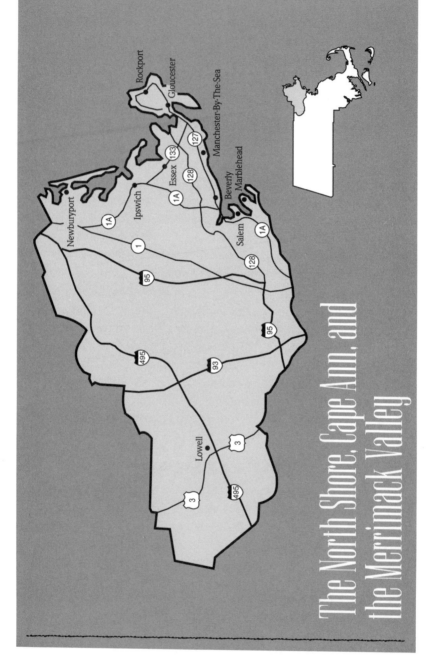

The North Shore, Cape Ann, and
the Merrimack Valley

The North Shore, Cape Ann, and the Merrimack Valley

The ragged coastline of the North Shore begins in the shipyards on Boston's north edges. As the crow flies, it stretches for 30 miles, up and around the island of Cape Ann, in and out of Ipswich Bay, and so along to the New Hampshire border. Along the way are the historic towns of Marblehead, Salem, Gloucester, Rockport, Ipswich, and Newburyport. Families flock to the museums of old Salem to hear the dark tales of the country's early history, retold here on-site and in chilling detail. Enchanting Marblehead's narrow streets and dollhouselike buildings stand in stark contrast to the workaday fishing villages of Gloucester and Rockport. Beautiful beaches and state parks bring families to Ipswich and Newburyport.

MARBLEHEAD

In the picturesque harbor town of Marblehead, the streets are so narrow and many of the buildings so small that the town resembles a scaled-down model, but it's a real place where real people live. Walk the twisting streets, eat seafood while you watch the boats, see a historic painting, and immerse yourselves in one of the best-preserved seaside villages in Massachusetts.

When you arrive in Marblehead, visit the **information booth** (62 Pleasant Street/Route 114, corner of Pleasant and Spring streets; 617–631–2868) to pick up a copy of the self-guided walking-tour brochure and to ask questions about the day's activities. The booth is open daily, 10:00 A.M.– 5:30 P.M., from Memorial Day through Columbus Day.

The prime tourist destination in Marblehead is **Abbot Hall** (Washington Square; 617–631–0528), a spired building that still operates as the town hall. After you come in the front door, walk through the lobby and then into the door on the left. You'll be confronted by an enormous painting, the original *Spirit of '76,* by Archibald Willard, given to the town by General John Devereaux in 1876, whose son was the model for the drummer boy. Open Monday, Thursday, and Friday, 8:00 A.M.–5:00 P.M.; Tuesday and Wednesday, 8:00 A.M.–9:00 P.M.; Saturday, 9:00 A.M.–6:00 P.M.; and Sunday, 11:00 A.M.–6:00 P.M. Free.

After you've seen the painting, follow the walking tour around Marblehead's narrow streets, ending up by the water. Watch the boats from **Clark Landing** (at the end of State Street) or from **Crocker Park** (off State Street). If you want to have a picnic lunch, there are two excellent sites to choose from: **Fort Sewall,** at the end of Front Street, and **Chandler Hovey Park,** at the end of Follett Street on the eastern end of Marblehead Neck, overlooking Marblehead Lighthouse and the harbor.

The Barnacle (141 Front Street; 617–631–4236) has great chowder and one of the best harbor views your family will see in Marblehead, unless you're lucky enough to know someone who owns one of the harborside mansions. If you're visiting Marblehead during the spring or summer, be sure to sit outside here; the balcony hangs right over the water. Lunch and dinner.

Unusual for a picturesque historic village like Marblehead, **Ten Mugford Street** (10 Mugford Street, Marblehead; 617–639–0343) is a reasonably priced B & B that's close to the harbor and beach area. There are five suites (two have kitchens) and three double rooms (these with shared bath). A washer and dryer are available to guests. Open year-round.

SALEM

Salem makes the most of its reputation as the location of the infamous Salem Witch Trials during the seventeenth century. But there's a lot more to it than the sad and rather gruesome witch stories: A topnotch waterfront area, a world-class museum, and a historic house with a secret stairway are among the highlights of Salem that have nothing to do with witches or trials.

KELLY'S TOP FAMILY ADVENTURES ON THE NORTH SHORE, CAPE ANN, AND IN THE MERRIMACK VALLEY

1. Parker River National Wildlife Refuge and Plum Island, Newburyport
2. Singing Beach, Manchester-by-the-Sea
3. Peabody and Essex Museums, Salem
5. Marblehead Harbor, especially during Race Week
6. Boott Cotton Mills, Lowell

When you arrive in Salem, go to the **Chamber of Commerce** (Old Town Hall, Front Street; 508–744–0004) for free self-guided tour maps and information about the day's activities.

If you'd rather let someone else do the driving (and that's not a bad idea in busy Salem), the **Salem Trolley Tours** (9 Pickering Way; 508–744–5469) are a good deal. The loop runs between Chestnut Street and Winter Island Park (a nice spot for a picnic). You can get on and off all day long, as you like, and the guide tells you what you're seeing. It runs March through November (weekends only in March). Fees are $8.00 for adults, $3.00 for kids five to twelve, and free for kids under five. Price includes discounts to some attractions.

Can't keep the kids away from the witch stories? Head for the **Salem Witch Museum** (19½ Washington Square; 508–744–1692) for the thirty-minute multimedia presentation about the witchcraft hysteria that gripped seventeenth-century Salem. The show is a bit scary and gruesome, and it is definitely *not* appropriate for kids under seven. Open daily, from September through June, 10:00 A.M.–5:00 P.M.; in July and August, 10:00 A.M.–7:00 P.M. Admission is $4.00 for adults and $2.50 for kids six through fourteen.

The **Salem Wax Museum of Witches and Seafarers** (Derby Street; 508–740–2929) does feature wax figures of life-size witches, but it also puts the witch stories in the context of Salem's seventeenth-century life as a major seaport, and it's not nearly as scary as the above. From November through June, it's open daily, 10:00 A.M.–4:30 P.M.; in July and August, open daily, 10:00 A.M.–6:00 P.M.; in October and November, open weekends, 10:00 A.M.–late in the evening (to serve the Halloween crowd). Admission is $4.00 for adults and $2.50 for kids fourteen and under.

Salem Maritime National Historic Site (174 Derby Street; 508–745–1470), on the waterfront, encompasses the Custom House, where Nathaniel Hawthorne worked, among other historic buildings. See the short slide show about Salem harbor, then take the self-guided tour of the Custom House. The weights and measures at the Scale House are especially fascinating to 1990s kids. They'll also enjoy watching demonstrations of the intricate skills required in shipbuilding. The site has been under renovative construction for several years; when the work is completed (sometime in 1996), you'll be able to tour fully restored warehouses as well as a three-masted square rigger. Open year-round, daily, 9:00 A.M.–5:00 P.M., except Thanksgiving, Christmas, and New Year's Day. Free admission.

If it wasn't in historic Salem, the **Peabody and Essex Museums** (East India Square; 508–745–9500 or 800–745–4054) would still be worth a special trip. The collection of items gathered by Salem sea captains on their round-the-world voyages is varied and eclectic, from elephant tusks to intricate navigational instruments to exotic plants to Chinese armor. The Asian art wing holds a superb collection of porcelain, furniture, and decorative arts. Try to take the free one-hour tour, given each day at 2:00 P.M. Open year-round, Monday through Saturday, 10:00 A.M.–5:00 P.M. (Thursday until 9:00 P.M.), and Sunday, noon –5:00 P.M.; closed Thanksgiving, Christmas, and New Year's Day. Admission is $7.00 for adults, $4.00 for kids six through sixteen; family discounts available.

The **House of the Seven Gables** (54 Turner Street; 508–744–0991) is a neat place to visit, even for people who aren't familiar with Nathaniel Hawthorne's book. Begin your visit by watching the short multimedia presentation of Hawthorne's story, then walk through the house to see the secret staircase, which winds up through a wall (this may be all that the younger kids will remember about the house), and the low-beamed attic. Hawthorne's birthplace is next door; it's furnished with original furniture, and the guides know a lot about the family and their times. In July and August, it's open daily, 9:30 A.M.–5:30 P.M.; in May, June, and September through December, open daily, 10:00 A.M.–4:30 P.M.; from January through April, open Monday through Saturday, 10:00 A.M.–4:30 P.M., and Sunday, noon–4:30 P.M.; closed the last two weeks of January and on Thanksgiving, Christmas, and New Year's Day. Admission is $6.50 for adults, $4.00 for kids ages thirteen through seventeen, and $3.00 for kids ages six through twelve.

Right next to the House of the Seven Gables is another venerable Salem attraction, **Harbor Sweets** (85 Leavitt Street; 508–745–7648). You can take a tour (impromptu; if you're interested in taking one, ask when you arrive) to see how this family-run business makes its delicious, preservative-free chocolates. Sweet Sloops are prized delicacies in Boston.

At the tip of a point that sticks out into Salem Bay, **Salem Willows Park** is a busy town park that's a fine destination for an afternoon of picnicking and outdoor activities. The views are good—Beverly's harbor on one side, the south coast of Cape Ann on the other. There's a small amusement park with a nice merry-go-round.

Amelia Payson Guest House (16 Winter Street; 508–744–8304) is a small B & B that's a pleasant home base if you want to spend more than one day exploring Salem. There are three rooms, all with private bath, and a studio apartment. Open year-round.

CAPE ANN

Connected to the mainland by a drawbridge, the rocky island of Cape Ann is a destination for families who don't mind driving an hour or so from Boston in order to reach some of eastern Massachusetts's less crowded tourist destinations.

In **Beverly** an afternoon of family vaudeville at **Marco the Magi's "Le Grand David and His Own Spectacular Magic Company"** (Cabot Street Cinema, 286 Cabot Street, Beverly; 508–927–3677) is in the don't-miss category. Even while you're waiting for the show to start, there's plenty to watch—jugglers and puppeteers keep the kids' fascination while attendees are taking their seats. The shows are quite long (about two and a half hours), but don't let their length dissuade you from bringing younger kids to see the magic shows, dancing, singing, and spectacular sets, all created by the dedicated resident stage troupe. From mid-September through July, performances are on Sunday from 3:00 (try to arrive about a half-hour early) to about 5:30 P.M. (with one intermission). From October through May, on holidays and most Saturdays, there's a two-hour magic show at the **Larcom Theatre** (14 Wallis Street; same phone number) at 1:30 P.M. (doors open at 1:00 P.M.). Admission is $10–$15 for either show. Buy tickets ahead at the Cabot Theatre box office, Monday through Saturday, 9:00 A.M.–9:00 P.M.

In Wenham, not far from Beverly, is the **Wenham Museum** (132 Main Street; 508–468–2377), which is often called "the doll museum" because of its enormous collection of dolls and dollhouses from around the world. Local children love to have their birthday parties here (by prior arrangement only). Open year-round (except early February), Monday through Friday, 11:00 A.M.–4:00 P.M.; Saturday 1:00–4:00 P.M.; and Sunday 2:00–5:00 P.M.; closed holidays. Admission is $3.00 for adults and $1.00 for children ages three to fourteen.

Manchester-by-the-Sea is home to one of the prettiest beaches on the North Shore, **Singing Beach,** a curving strip of sand that "sings" when the waves stroke it just right. Day-trippers from Boston take the train from North Station and walk the mile (a pleasant walk) to the beach. Between Memorial Day and Labor Day, beachside parking is strictly limited to residents only, so you'll have to drop the family at the beach, then drive back into town to park in one of the designated areas. At the beach you'll find a snack stand, rest rooms, and changing rooms. On the way to the beach, you'll pass a grocery store that's perfectly located for last-minute picnic fixings, and there's a good ice cream shop right next door, too, for postbeach snacking. Directions: Take Route 128 North from Boston, toward Gloucester. Take exit 15 (Pine Street). Turn right, go through the village of Manchester-by-the-Sea, and turn right onto Central Street, which ends at Singing Beach.

From Manchester it's a short drive north on Route 128 to **Gloucester,** a grittier seaside village that's well known for its expert fishermen. Most members of the family will recognize the often-reproduced **Fishermen's Statue,** near the drawbridge. The statue, called The Man at the Wheel, was commissioned in 1923 to celebrate the town's 300th anniversary. Drive along the Harbor Loop to see the workings of a busy harbor; stop at the **Gloucester Marine Railways Corporation** to see boats being repaired.

Built in 1926 by John Hays Hammond, an inventor, **Hammond Castle Museum** (80 Hesperus Avenue, Gloucester; 508–283–2081) is an odd combination of the very old—bits of medieval French houses are built right into the building's walls—and the modern, for its day: The eight-story, 8,600-pipe organ is the largest organ in a private home in the country. Most tours include a short demonstration of the organ, which is now played by a computer. There are lots of other sights here, from a huge fifteenth-century fireplace to a glass-enclosed courtyard to a swimming pool that Hammond regularly dove into from his bedroom window. During the summer the castle is open daily, 10:00 A.M.–5:00 P.M.; otherwise, the castle is open Wednesday through Sunday, 10:00 A.M.–5:00 P.M. *Note:* During the summer you'll guide yourselves via the self-guided tour brochure, but during the rest of the year you'll have to take the forty-five-minute guided tour. Admission is $5.00 for adults, $3.00 for kids six through twelve, and free for kids under six.

Good Harbor Beach is the most popular swimming beach in Gloucester. It's on Thatcher Road. Parking costs $15 (arrive early or you may not get a spot).

Overlooking Good Harbor Beach is **Samarkand Guest House** (1 Harbor Road, Gloucester; 508–283–3757), a homey, family-oriented B & B that's been here for thirty years. Rates run $45–$85.

At the mouth of the Annisquam River, **Wingaersheek Beach** (Atlantic Street, Gloucester; no phone) is a small sandy beach that's an especially good destination for families with small children: they love climbing on the smooth rocks and dunes. From Route 128 take exit 13.

Halibut Point Restaurant and Pub (289 Main Street; 508–281–1900) has good chowder and lots of locals: Head to the back room, which is more appropriate for families than the louder pub area up front.

The Rudder, on Rocky Neck (73 Rocky Neck Avenue; 508–283–7967) is a family-run restaurant whose fun-loving owners often provide unorthodox entertainment along with their excellent food. Sit outside on the deck overlooking Smith Cove during warm weather. If you're lucky, you'll be treated to a baton-twirling show by one of owner Evie's daughters, and on extra-special days Evie tells hilarious versions of nursery rhymes. Lunch and dinner are served daily from spring through fall.

Up the road in Rockport, another hardworking fishing village, the quirky **Paper House** (50 Pigeon Hill Street; Rockport; 508–546–2629) is worth a stop. Everything in the house, from the walls to the furnishings, is made from paper. Open daily in July and August, 10:00 A.M.–5:00 P.M. Admission is $1.00 for adults and 50 cents for kids six to fourteen.

Halibut Point Reservation (Gott Avenue, Rockport; 508–546–2297) is a lovely place for walking and picnicking by the sea. It's not a sandy beach, though; the shore here is rocky, and kids should be encouraged to keep their shoes on to avoid cutting their feet on rocks or shells. Take a twenty-minute walk around the old quarry (hang onto the kids' hands), then play in the tide pools. Bring windbreakers and warm clothes —it's usually windy—and keep an eye out for poison ivy. Open year-round, daily, 8:00 A.M.-sunset. Parking costs $5.00.

Just a few minutes from Halibut Point is the **Old Farm Inn** (291 Granite Street, Rockport; 508–546–3237), a B & B that's a great summer getaway for families. There are ten guest rooms in the three buildings (a main house, a barn, and a cottage), all with private bath and some with a refrigerator. Most of the rooms can be arranged in family-style suites, and cribs, cots, and rollaway beds are available. An extended continental breakfast is included in all room rates. Open April through December.

NORTH OF CAPE ANN

The **Ipswich River Wildlife Sanctuary** (Perkins Row, Topsfield; 508–887–9264) has 25 miles of trails on 2,400 acres of land that are protected by the Massachusetts Audubon Society. Start your visit at the information center, where you can pick up a trail map. For families the best trail is one that leads to the **Rockery,** a pile of enormous boulders that kids love to climb up, through, into, and over. Continue on around the pond (look for ducks, turtles, and frogs) and then around the marsh, from which you can look over the wetlands of Topsfield and Ipswich. The sanctuary is open

KELLY'S TOP ANNUAL EVENTS ON THE NORTH SHORE

Salem Seaport Festival, May, Salem; (617) 262–1414

Strawberry Festival, June, Meetinghouse Green, Ipswich;
(508) 356–3231

St. Peter's Fiesta, late June, Gloucester; (508) 283–1601

Castle Hill Festival, June through September, Ipswich;
(508) 356–4351

The Children's Theatre at Maudslay State Park, June through
September, Curzon's Mill Road, Newburyport;
(508) 465–7223

Marblehead Race Week, late July; (617) 631–2868

Hammond Castle Medieval Festival, July, Gloucester;
(508) 283–2080

Gloucester Waterfront Festival, August, Gloucester;
(617) 283–1601

Essex Clamfest, September, Memorial Park; (508) 283–1601

Salem's Haunted Happenings, October, Salem; (508) 744–0004

Christmas on Cape Ann, December, Rockport, Gloucester,
Manchester, and Essex; (508) 283–1601

year-round from Tuesday through Sunday, dawn to dusk. Admission is $3.00 for adults and free for kids. *Note:* Don't bring your dog; this is a wildlife sanctuary. Do bring bug repellent, especially during the spring.

Here's an unusual day trip: On a warm summer day, it's fun to take the boat from Rockport harbor to **Thacher Island,** where your family can spend the day walking the trails and rocky beaches, climbing up the old lighthouse for an even better view, and enjoying nature without having to worry about cars or fences getting in the way. On good-weather days the boat (508–546–2326) leaves **T-Wharf** twice a day, at 9:00 A.M. and 1:00 P.M. The last trip back to Rockport is at 4:00 P.M. You must bring fresh water with you—there's none on the island—as well as warm clothes, since the temperature is usually twenty degrees cooler on the island than on the mainland. Show up early; it's first come, first served, and there are no reservations.

Crane Beach (Argilla Road, Ipswich; 508–356–4354 for recorded info and 508–356–4351 for a person) is a long, clean beach that's great for swimming, picnicking, and walking—as long as the greenhead flies aren't around. These flies, common from mid-July to about mid-August, are so pesky that the beach office has a recorded line for you to call to find out whether or not the flies are around. During the summer there are lifeguards on duty and the bathhouse and snack bar are open. There are several pleasant, easy walks to take from the beach. One leads to Castle Hill (more follows); the other is a self-guided nature walk (pick up a booklet for $2.00 at the gate) that leads you over boardwalks, through a swamp, and into a piney forest. Open year-round. The parking fee, which includes beach admission for all passengers, is as follows: Memorial Day through Labor Day, $3.00 per car on Monday and Tuesday, $6.00 per car on Wednesday through Friday, and $10.00 per car on weekends; spring and fall, $3.25 per car on weekdays and $3.75 per car on weekends; winter, $2.75 per car on weekdays and $3.25 on weekends. *Note:* No dogs, please. *Directions:* From Route 1A south of Ipswich, take Route 133 East. Turn left onto Northgate Road. At the end of this road, turn right onto Argilla Road, which ends at the beach.

Castle Hill (508–356–4351) is the former home of the Crane family, for whom Crane Beach is named. Now owned and managed by the Trustees of Reservations, a private land trust whose holdings include many other properties listed in this book, the beautiful old mansion is the summer home to an excellent performing arts series. Audiences sit on the sweeping lawn to hear the music or watch the play. Call or write ahead for a schedule; tickets sometimes sell out.

At **New England Alive** (163 High Street, corner of Routes 1A and 133, Ipswich; 508–356–7013), kids can hold baby birds in their hands and learn about domestic and wild animals, including a black bear and several large reptiles. What makes this petting-zoo type of animal park unique is that it's also a wild-animal hospital and orphanage. Picnicking is encouraged; there are plenty of outdoor tables on the shady grounds. Open May through November: weekdays, 10:00 A.M.–5:00 P.M., and weekends, 9:30 A.M.–6:00 P.M. Admission is $5.00 for adults, $3.00 for kids two through twelve, and free for kids under two.

Wolf Hollow (114 Essex Road, Route 133; 508–356–0216) is yet another wild-animal refuge, this one dedicated to the gray wolf. Open to the public on weekends only, 1:00–5:00 P.M., year-round. *Note:* Try to see the presentations at 1:30 P.M. (also at 3:30 P.M. from March through November). Admission is $3.00 for adults, $2.50 for kids.

Goodale Orchards (123 Argilla Road, Ipswich; 508–356–5366) is more than an orchard—it has a swing in the barn, animals in the barnyard who are accustomed to being petted, and hayrides during the fall. In season pick your own strawberries, blueberries, raspberries, apples, and pumpkins. Don't leave without buying a few of the delicious homemade doughnuts. Open daily from mid-May through December, 9:00 A.M.–6:00 P.M., and weekends in April, 9:00 A.M.–6:00 P.M.

Foote Brothers Canoe Rental (Topsfield Road, Ipswich; 508–356–9771) provides canoes and advice for families who enjoy paddling on a calm river.

Essex is the self-proclaimed home of the fried clam. Locals and tourists alike crowd into **Woodman's** (121 Main Street/Route 133; 508–768–6451), where, according to the Woodman family, the first clam was breaded and fried in 1916.

The **Essex Shipbuilding Museum** (28 Main Street/Route 133W, Essex; 508–786–7541) is a remnant of the days when more wooden ships came from Essex than from anywhere else in the world. This excellent small museum not only shows you how the ships were built but also gives you the context you need to understand the significance of the industry to the area. Real tools allow kids to try their hand at shipbuilding. Open from May 15 through October 15, Thursday through Sunday, 11:00 A.M.–4:00 P.M., and by appointment year-round. Admission is $2.00 for adults and kids over twelve, and free for kids under twelve.

Essex is also known as an antiques-lover's haven. One of the more interesting shops is the **White Elephant** (32 Main Street; 508–768–6901), next door to the Shipbuilding Museum. The stock changes often, but in the past has included collections of wooden teeth, old train sets, and wasp-waisted dresses from a hundred years ago. Open daily, year-round.

Parker River National Wildlife Refuge (Northern Boulevard, Newburyport; 508–465–5753), which covers about two-thirds of **Plum Island,** is a favorite destination for Boston-area families. The refuge is operated by the U.S. Fish and Wildlife Service; it is one of the very few natural barrier beach, dune, and salt marsh complexes left on the coast of New England. Along with the abundant wildlife on view here in its natural habitat, the great attraction of Plum Island (which is what the locals call it) is the beach. Those who are in the know arrive at the refuge very early (before 9:00 A.M.), since only a few parking spots are available. There are several observation towers that are well-used by bird-watchers in March and April, the peak migration periods for ducks and other waterfowl; the views are always good, though, and there are always birds to see—300 (or so) species live in the area. The 6-mile-long beach is nearly always deserted. Note, however, that because of the strong undertow, it's not a good place for families with small children, and everyone should be especially careful here because there are no lifeguards. During the plovers' nesting season (early April through early June), the beach is usually closed. Otherwise open year-round, daily, from dawn to dusk. Parking costs $5.00 per car. *Note:* Don't bring pets; do bring bug spray.

Also in Newburyport is **Maudslay State Park** (Curzon's Mill Road; 508–465–7223). When the mansion of this 500-acre estate was taken down in the 1950s, the landscaped grounds became a state park. It's a great place on a spring or summer afternoon—picnic spots abound, and there are lots of walking trails through formal gardens, rolling meadows, piney woods, and an enormous stand of mountain laurel. Open year-round; free.

A gracious inn that's also entirely appropriate for families, the **Clark Currier Inn** (45 Green Street, Newburyport; 508–465–8363) is a classic 1803 Federal building that's not far from the main shopping area of Newburyport. Be sure to request a family-style room; though they're all large, not all the bedrooms are appropriate for children. There's a comfortable lounge/TV room, and the backyard and garden (complete with a picturesque gazebo) are a welcome sight for kids who need to run around a bit. Open year-round.

LOWELL

The main tourist attraction of the Merrimack Valley is Lowell, the country's first planned industrial city, in whose enormous brick mills the world's first mass-produced cotton cloth originated. **Lowell National Historic Park** (visitor center at Market Mills, 246 Market Street; 508–970–5000) provides excellent presentations and tours that bring Lowell's heyday to life—in some cases, deafeningly so.

Lowell was named for Francis Cabot Lowell, the man who came up with the idea (and much of the money) for a planned industrial community. He also had the idea, highly radical in its time, of employing women, who made up the majority of the workforce. Kirk Boott headed up the group of people who planned, financed, and built Lowell. The largest of the cotton mills was named for him, and today the **Boott Cotton Mills**

Learn about the textile industry at Lowell's Boott Cotton Mills Museum.
(Photo by Kindra Clineff/Courtesy Massachusetts Office of Travel and Tourism)

Museum is the star of Lowell. Restored in 1992, the museum re-creates the work environment that the "mill girls" experienced, complete with eighty-eight looms in full operation. Earplugs are available for tourists, but there was no such thing for the workers, who spent about seventy-two hours a week here, on their feet, without the benefit of ventilation, and earning a weekly wage of $2.25. History comes to life here in more ways than one: Be sure to listen to the recorded stories of some of the workers who ran the mills.

Another highlight of a family trip to Lowell is the **boat ride** through the city's intricate canal-and-lock system. Reservations for these tours are strongly recommended; you wouldn't want to arrive in Lowell to find out that your family won't fit onto any boats that day. Tours leave from the visitor center (508–970–5000). The fee for the boat is $3.00 for adults, $1.00 for kids age six to sixteen, and free for under-fives.

Papillon means "butterfly" in French, and that's what your family will see at the **Butterfly Place at Papillon Park** (120 Tyngsboro Park, Westford; 508–392–0955), a highly unusual farm where hundreds of butterflies flutter above and through flowering plants and weeds in an enormous solar dome. It's fun to see how many different kinds of butterflies you can identify. There's a pleasant picnic spot, too. Open daily from mid-April through mid-October, 10:00 A.M.–5:00 P.M. If you want to avoid the chaotic days when school groups crowd the dome, call ahead. Admission is $5.00 for adults, $4.00 for kids three to twelve, and free for kids under three.

Central Massachusetts

Rolling hills make up most of this peaceful area of the state, a region that Boston-area families treasure as a nearby source of seasonal rural activities. In spring, pastures are full of young animals kicking up their heels. Clear lakes and large parks welcome picnickers on summer afternoons. The city of Worcester has several good family-oriented museums. Orchards provide hours of fun for enthusiastic apple-pickers from mid-September through early November. Quiet country roads lead to the hiking and cross-country skiing trails that crisscross the region.

South of Worcester, Old Sturbridge Village is an early nineteenth-century-era "village" that was constructed in 1946. Unpaved roads, period-costumed "interpreters," and working artisans give kids a flavor of what it might have been like to visit a typical New England village during the first fifty years of the Republic. The nearby Publick House is a terrific base for exploring the area; the hotel's family-oriented Winter Weekend packages are a bargain.

THE NASHOBA VALLEY

A hilly region that's served Bostonians as an easy escape for well over a century, the Nashoba Valley hasn't changed much since the Alcott family set up a commune in Harvard with other transcendentalists in 1843.

The **Toy Cupboard Theater and Museum** (57 East George Hill Road, Lancaster; 508–365–9519) displays early marionettes, antique

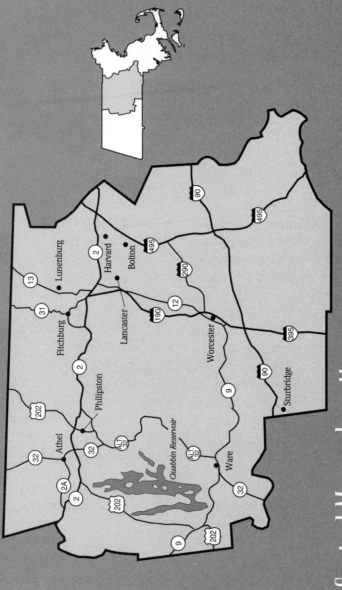

Central Massachusetts

dolls, and children's books by John Greene Chandler (*The Remarkable Story of Chicken Little*). The main draw here is the extraordinary puppet shows, most of which are based on well-known fairy tales. Puppet shows take place in July and August at 2:00 and 3:30 P.M. on Wednesday, Thursday, and usually Saturday and Sunday; call ahead. Shows are about a half-hour long. The museum is open on weekend afternoons during July and August.

The 200-acre property surrounding **Fruitlands Museum and Farmhouse** (102 Prospect Hill Road, Harvard; 508–456–3924) provides stunning views of the Nashua River Valley and, in the far distance, of mountains in southern New Hampshire. On a clear day you may be able to see as far as southern New Hampshire. The museum is dedicated to the memory of the transcendentalists, many of whom spent seven months of 1843 in the farmhouse at the bottom of the hill. The transcendentalists believed that God exists in humans and nature alike. Their beliefs led them to a distinct "back-to-nature" lifestyle, very unusual during their time.

Story time is fun time at the Fruitlands Museum. (Courtesy Fruitlands Museum)

They tried living in a communal building on a farm where they could be as self-sufficient as possible. They wore simple linen clothing, adopted a vegetarian diet, and spent much of their time outdoors. Among them were the Alcott family (Louisa, her three sisters, and her parents).

The group gave its communal home the hopeful name of Fruitlands in the expectation that its orchards would produce an abundance of fruit. Unfortunately, the site wasn't optimal, so the trees didn't provide as much sustenance as the group had hoped. For this reason and others, its members left Harvard and went back to Concord.

In 1910 Clara Endicott Sears purchased the property, which was quite run-down. She restored the farmhouse and opened it as a museum in honor of the Alcotts and their friends Emerson, Thoreau, and Margaret Fuller. The building houses mementos of the group. Also on the property is a museum dedicated to Harvard's Shaker community (which donated journals and an office building to Miss Sears). A small museum holds Thoreau's arrowhead collection, among other interesting artifacts of the Native Americans who once lived in the area. The museums are open from mid-May to mid-October, Tuesday through Sunday, 10:00 A.M.–5:00 P.M. Admission is $6.00 for adults and $2.50 for kids.

One of the best pick-your-own orchards is **Doe's** (327 Ayer Road, Harvard; 508–772–4139). The trees are old and big; the Doe family planted the first trees in 1915, and many families have been coming from near and far since then.

Nashoba Valley Winery and Orchards (100 Wattaquadoc Hill Road, Bolton; 508–779–5521) is more expensive than other orchards, but that's probably because the owners expend more effort on landscaping here than most orchard-keepers do. Pick berries during the summer and early fall, apples throughout the fall, and be sure to bring a picnic. In the winter it's a nice place to cross-country ski. Regardless of the season, you can take a tour of the winery, where the owner makes fruit and berry wines (samples available for grown-ups during the tour—unusual and delicious; try the dry blueberry). Tours cost $1.00 for adults and are free for kids. Open year-round; twenty-minute tours are given Friday through Sunday, 11:00 A.M.–5:00 P.M.

GREATER WORCESTER

The second largest city in Massachusetts as well as New England, Worcester loses a lot of tourists to Boston, but it's managed to build quite a busy cultural life for itself with several good museums.

One such stop is **John Woodman Higgins Armory** (100 Barber Avenue, Worcester; 508–853–6015). Try on a helmet—or perhaps a full suit of armor, if you're big enough—at this remarkable collection of arms and armor, the largest in the Western Hemisphere. The orientation is fun for everyone; the interpreter selects a visitor to "suit up," encouraging her or him to describe how uncomfortable and restrictive the armor actually is. The Quest Gallery has costumes for everyone: princesses and princes, queens and kings, and helmets for moms and dads. The museum runs interesting workshops for kids in which they learn to make gargoyles, books, masks, pennants, and shields. Chess games are always going on in the Quest Gallery. Open year-round. Tuesday through Saturday, 10:00 A.M.–4:00 P.M., and Sunday, noon–4:00 P.M.; in July and August, open Monday, 1:00–4:00 P.M.; closed most holidays. Admission is $4.75 for adults, $3.75 for kids six to sixteen, and free for kids under six.

Worcester Art Museum (55 Salisbury Street, Worcester; 508–799–4406). Nearly every period of art is featured in this small, excellent city museum. Highlights include a sixth-century floor mosaic in the central court area; a twelfth-century Romanesque house that was moved here, stone by stone, from France; an eleven-headed, ninth-century Japanese sculpture; and an extensive collection of pre-Columbian sculpture in various media, including gold and ceramic. The restaurant serves light snacks and lunches. A garden cafe is open during the summer. Open year-round, Tuesday through Friday, 11:00 A.M.–4:00 P.M.; Saturday, 10:00 A.M.–5:00 P.M.; and Sunday 1:00–5:00 P.M.; closed major holidays. Admission is $4.00 for adults and free for kids under eighteen; free admission on Saturday from 10:00 A.M. to noon.

The focus at **New England Science Center** (222 Harrington Way, Worcester; 508–791–9211) is on live animals. There's a small zoo with large animals, such as polar bears and big cats; if your kids aren't bothered by seeing animals enclosed in chain-link fences, you'll probably enjoy the short train ride that takes you past their pens. Inside the three-story building are several good interactive exhibits, three large aquariums, and a good planetarium show. Open year-round, Monday through Saturday, 10:00 A.M.–5:00 P.M., and Sunday, noon–5:00 P.M. Admission is $6.00 for adults and $4.00 for kids three to sixteen.

An old-fashioned amusement park, **Whalom Park** (Route 13, Lunenburg; 508–342–3707) isn't huge, and there are nearly as many kiddie rides as adults-only rides. Clowns wander the premises, and there's a parade every day. Some adults might be nervous on the slightly rickety roller coasters; if this sounds like too much for you, stick to the rides that are closer to the ground. Other attractions include a water slide, a minigolf course, and paddleboats and swimming in the lake on weekends. The shady, grassy picnic area is very pleasant. Open April through September, Tuesday through Sunday, noon–10:00 P.M. Admission is $2.99 per person. All rides, all day: From April through mid-May and after Labor Day, $6.99 per person; otherwise, $9.99 ($12.99 including the water slide). Kiddie Land only: $6.99. If you enter the park after 5:00 P.M., all rides are $5.99 per person.

Perhaps you will get a chance to suit up at the Higgins Armory Museum.
(Photo by Chuck Kidd)

KELLY'S TOP FAMILY ADVENTURES IN CENTRAL MASSACHUSETTS

1. Old Sturbridge Village, Sturbridge
2. Quabbin Reservoir and Park, Ware and Belchertown
3. Fruitlands Museum and Farmhouse, Harvard
4. Apple-picking in Harvard

Quabbin Reservoir and Park (485 Ware Road, entrance on Route 9 between Ware and Belchertown; 413–323–7221) is a protected watershed for the Quabbin Reservoir, which supplies water to 2.4 million of the residents of Massachusetts. The man-made watershed lands also supply wilderness, wildlife, forest, research, historical, and recreational resources. The visitor center is located at Winsor Dam, about 2 miles from Route 9, and provides information about the many hiking trails on the eighty-seven-square-mile reservation and a few exhibits about the reservoir's construction. The reservoir was begun in 1926; the towns of Dana, Prescott, Greenwich, and Enfield were "discontinued," which means that the state bought the land from the residents and moved them away, then flooded the land. **Enfield Lookout,** up a winding road after you cross the dam, overlooks a spectacular view of the reservoir and the hills that were once the town of Enfield. A good, though hilly, walk begins across the road from the lookout. If your family wants to walk on the reservoir's trails, do take the time to stop at the visitor center to pick up maps. Fishing and boating are at designated areas only (the northern end of the reservoir). Please, no dogs, swimming, off-road vehicles, sliding on dams, or cross-country skiing.

Brookfield Orchards (12 Lincoln Road, North Brookfield; 508–867–6858) is a 200-acre orchard that's open year-round. Come in the spring to see the apple blossoms, during the summer for early apples (mid-July for some varieties), throughout the fall for pick-your-own apples, and in the winter for cross-country skiing at **Brookfield Orchards Touring Center** (12 kilometers of trails). The country store features maple syrup, cheeses, lots of apple products, and penny candy. There's a small playground, too.

Not far from Brookfield is the pretty little town of Philipston, where there's a nicely maintained cross-country ski area, **Red Apple Farm Touring Center** (Highland Avenue, off Route 2A, Philipston; 508–249–6763). Ten miles of trails are here.

Douglas State Forest and Wallum Lake (Wallum Lake Road, Douglas; 508–476–7872) is an enormous state forest—nearly 4,000 acres—with a plethora of picnic sites and a big lake that's mercifully divided between pleasure-boat users and swimmers. The beach has a good bathhouse and lifeguards. Open Memorial Day weekend through Labor Day. Parking is $5.00 per car.

If the kids are into animals, they'll love a visit to **Southwick's Wild Animal Farm** (off Route 16, Mendon; 508–883–9182), where they're likely to see giraffes, peacocks, alligators, and more than a hundred other species of animals on a 300-acre farm. There's a petting zoo, of course, and kids can take rides on ponies, elephants, and sometimes camels. During the summer there's a short, circus type of show every day. In April, May, September, and October, it's open on weekends, 10:00 A.M.–5:00 P.M.; from Memorial Day through Labor Day, open daily, 10:00 A.M.–5:00 P.M. Admission is $7.00 for adults, $5.00 for kids three to twelve, and free for kids under three.

The deep chasm at **Purgatory Chasm State Reservation** (Purgatory Road, Sutton; 508–278–6486) is a dramatic sight and a nice spot to hike at any time of year, but in the summer the cool, damp air is especially pleasant. A marked path leads down the series of ravines that form the chasm. Note that this path, rough and steep in spots, isn't appropriate for kids under ten. There are picnic spots galore in the reservation, as well as a good playground area and a short marked path through the woods that's more appropriate for younger kids. Open year-round, dawn to dusk. Parking costs $5.00 per car.

The Indian name for **Webster Lake** (off Routes 16 and 193, Webster) is Lake Chargoggagogmanchauggagoggchaubunagungamaugg. Not

A hands-on day of fun awaits at Southwick's Wild Animal Farm. (Courtesy Southwick Zoo)

surprisingly, this is the longest geographic name in the United States. Rough translation: I fish on my side of the lake, you fish on yours, and no one fishes in between.

One of the best—and largest—outdoor living history museum-villages in the country, **Old Sturbridge Village** (1 Old Sturbridge Village Road, Sturbridge; 508–347–3362) is worth at least one full day's visit for any family. The village re-creates the daily life of a rural inland community in the 1830s with its farms, fields, shops, houses, and outlying mill areas. More than forty buildings from all over New England were carefully dismantled and transported here in the mid-1940s, then painstakingly reassembled and furnished in period style. The period portrayed by the village is particularly significant because it was a time when New Englanders' lives were transformed by the rise of commerce and manufacturing, improvements in agriculture and transportation, emigration and growing urbanization, and the political and social changes of a prospering young country.

Younger children will enjoy seeing the costumed interpreters who set the scene, as well as the animals, the unpaved streets, and the interesting simple tools and machines that the interpreters use. Older kids will enjoy the interaction with the interpreters, who welcome questions and participation in many activities (for a fee), such as sheep shearing, spinning, weaving, gardening, fireplace cooking, tinsmithing, watercolor painting, and candlemaking.

Note: Advance registration is required for all fee-based activities. Wear comfortable shoes; the unpaved streets can be hard on the feet after a while. A stroller will be a lifesaver if you have a small child, though you'll have to leave the stroller outside at many of the buildings. The village is remarkably accessible for visitors with disabilities. More than half of the buildings are wheelchair accessible, and the unpaved roads are generally firm, stable, and level. Sign-language interpreters are available by prior arrangement.

From January 1 through February 18, the facility is open weekends only, 10:00 A.M.–4:00 P.M., plus February 19. From February 20 through March 31, it's open Tuesday through Sunday, 10:00 A.M.–4:00 P.M. From April 1 through October 26, it's open daily, 9:00 A.M.–5:00 P.M. From October 27 through December 31, it's open Tuesday through Sunday, 10:00 A.M.–4:00 P.M. It's also open November 4, November 11, and December 30; closed Christmas and New Year's Day. Admission (good for two consecutive days) is $15.00 for adults, $7.50 for kids six to fifteen, and free for kids under six.

The Publick House and Colonel Ebenezer Crafts Inn (Route 131 on Sturbridge Common, Sturbridge; 508–347–3313) is a large complex of accommodations that cater to Sturbridge Village visitors, families from the Boston area who need a quick getaway, and long-distance drivers who know about the restaurant. The Publick House opened in 1771; the original building is vintage colonial, with wide plank floors. The Country Motor Lodge is modern, with larger rooms and bathrooms, and the Chamberlain House has suite-type accommodations. A mile away, out of the bustle of "downtown" Sturbridge, the more gracious Crafts Inn has exquisitely painted wood paneling in the guest rooms, which are furnished with four-poster beds, and a library and lounge area. All guests have access to the pool, tennis courts, and playground at the Publick House.

KELLY'S TOP ANNUAL EVENTS IN CENTRAL MASSACHUSETTS

Washington's Birthday Celebration, February, Old Sturbridge
Village; (508) 347-3362

Athol-to-Orange River Rat Race, April, Athol; (413) 249-3849

Eastern Sprints Regatta rowing championships, May, Lake
Quinsigamond, Quinsigamond State Park, Worcester;
(508) 757-2140

The Brimfield Flea Market, May, July (Independence Day weekend), and September (Labor Day weekend), Brimfield
Common; (413) 283-6149 or (413) 283-2418

Harvest Weekend, September, Old Sturbridge Village;
(508) 347-3362

Pumpkin Commission Weigh-In and Festival, October,
Phillipston; (413) 249-3849

Thanksgiving at Old Sturbridge Village, November,
Old Sturbridge Village; (508) 347-3362

Falconry Demonstrations at the Higgins Armory Museum,
November, Worcester; (508) 853-6015

Room rates are $70–$150. Bargain packages are available during the Yankee Winter Weekends (January-March), which usually include admission to Old Sturbridge Village.

The **Publick House Restaurant** is a six-dining-room complex that includes the original low-ceilinged tavern. The cathedral-ceiling main dining room features huge, heavy chandeliers. The fare is hearty: thick chops, pot roast, individually baked lobster pie, and Indian pudding for dessert. Kid-size portions are available. The service is excellent. Open for breakfast, lunch, and dinner year-round.

Charlie Brown's Steak House (Haynes Street, Sturbridge; 508–347–5559) accommodates much of the run-off crowd from the Publick House restaurant in a family-friendly atmosphere. There are lots of booths that are great for corraling the kids, and the whimsical decor gives them something to look at. Some of the booths look like chicken coops, a bike hangs from the ceiling, and farm tools are sprinkled throughout the dining areas. The menu features mesquite-grilled burgers, swordfish, and salmon, as well as good fried chicken and seafood pies. Open daily, year-round, for lunch and dinner and for Sunday brunch.

Sturbridge Host (Route 20, Sturbridge; 508–347–7393 or 800–582–3232) is another option in Sturbridge, this one directly across from Old Sturbridge Village. It's also a conference center, so don't be surprised if you see large groups of similarly dressed conventioneers milling about. The decor is faux colonial and the furniture is reproduction colonial, but it's all very comfortable, if a bit sanitized. You can't beat the location, though, and the amenities are great: there's an indoor pool, a sauna, a health club and exercise room, tennis, minigolf, and, on Cedar Lake, boating and fishing. Rates run $85–$150.

Like many other places that serve the crowds who flock to Old Sturbridge Village, **Rom's** (Route 131, Sturbridge; 508–347–3349) seems as though it's been here forever. It has, practically; it began as a sandwich stand twenty-five years ago and gradually expanded to its present incarnation as an enormous restaurant (six dining rooms) that serves good classic meals, such as pizza, open-faced sandwiches, and veal parmesan, at reasonable prices. Open year-round for lunch and dinner.

Just a few miles southwest of Sturbridge, **Misty Meadows** (Allen Hill Road, Holland; 413–245–7466) is a three-bedroom B & B with pretty furnishings, hospitable innkeepers, and very reasonable rates—$48 for a double room. Please call ahead.

Salem Cross Inn (Route 9, West Brookfield; 508–867–2345) is named for the cross on the front door latch that was placed there to fend off witchcraft when the building went up in 1720. It was built by a grandson of Peregrine White, the only baby born on board the *Mayflower*. The main dining room has a low ceiling, dark wood beams, and dim lighting in the evening. The view out the back windows are of the sweeping lawns and fields that surround the building. The menu changes with the season. During the winter, roasts are cooked on a roasting jack and breads are baked in a genuine beehive oven. A spring or summer evening might feature a roast cooked outdoors over a pit, served with chowder. The year-round dinner menu includes, surprisingly, Middle Eastern fare (the owners are Syrian) and, unsurprisingly, such standards as shrimp cocktail and a good relish tray. The children's menu always has three choices, and kids can also order half-portions of anything on the menu for $1.00 less than the regular price. Open year-round, Tuesday and Friday, 11:30 A.M.–9:00 P.M.; Saturday, 5:00–10:00 P.M.; and Sunday, noon–9:00 P.M.

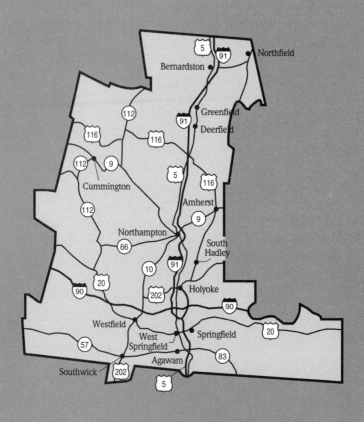

Northfield

5 91

Bernardston

112

116 I-91 Greenfield

116 Deerfield

112 9

Cummington

5

116

112

Amherst

Northampton 9

66 South
Hadley

10 I-91

20 202 Holyoke

90 202 90

Westfield 20

57 West Springfield

Southwick 202 Agawam 83

5

The Pioneer Valley

The Pioneer Valley

The Pioneer Valley borders the Connecticut River, which stretches north to south through the state. The river valley is broad and fertile, making it excellent farming country. Many crops are raised here, including corn, tobacco, and sod for golf courses. The area was one of the first regions of inland New England to be secured by English settlers during the turbulent late seventeenth and early eighteenth centuries, when they battled Native American tribes and French militia. The town of Deerfield is one of the best sources of information about this early period of colonial history. At Turners Falls there's an interesting underwater view of a fish ladder, where salmon and shad swim during the spring. In Agawam, Riverside Park is New England's largest amusement park. It features all the essentials—roller coasters, bumper cars, water rides, stock car races, and lots of sticky fried food. Finally, for twelve days every September, the Big E (the Eastern States Exhibition), in Springfield, is the biggest annual fair on the East Coast. It's family fare all the way—livestock shows, crafts contests, musical entertainment, rides, and midways.

NORTHFIELD AND BERNARDSTON

The historic village of Bernardston boasts several buildings on the National Register of Historic Places, including the library, the Unitarian Church, the town halls, and the old high school, all of which are on Main Street. **Falls River Inn** (junction of Routes 5 and 10, Bernardston; 413–648–9904) is a big old three-story hotel with seven guest rooms, all with private bath, most with claw-foot tubs, and some with fireplaces. Breakfast is served in the large main dining room; dinner is available here as well as in the smaller dining rooms, where working fireplaces warm diners during the winter. This is a great spot to spend a night or two if your family is skiing or enjoying the other outdoor activities available at nearby Northfield Mountain. Rates are $62–$68 per night, double occupancy, including full breakfast.

Also in Bernardston, **Four Leaf Clover** (Route 5; 413–648–9514) is a smaller, more family-oriented restaurant that's open for lunch and dinner year-round.

Underneath Northfield Mountain is **Northfield Mountain Recreation and Environmental Center** (99 Millers Falls Road, off Route 63, Northfield; 413–659–3714), an enormous power-generating facility that's owned by Northeast Utilities. Atop the mountain is a water reservoir that's used to generate power when consumer demand exceeds other power sources. Since the utility company's interest is in what's under and on top of the mountain, they've graciously opened their hillside property to outdoor recreation enthusiasts. The altitude makes for fairly consistent snow on the 25 miles of cross-country skiing trails, which in warm weather are used for hiking. The lodge offers ski and snowshoe rentals and lessons. You can rent canoes at **Barton Cove,** on the Connecticut River. There's a campground at Barton Cove, too (413–863–9300 for reservations).

The *Quinnetukut II* (Route 63, Northfield; 413–659–3714) takes passengers on short cruises on the Connecticut River between Northfield and Gill. Knowledgeable guides comment on the flora, fauna, and history of the areas you pass through. Boats leave from the River View area, across from the entrance to Northfield Mountain. Reservations are necessary.

GREENFIELD AND TURNERS FALLS

From Greenfield drive through the small town of Montague to reach **Turners Falls,** the site of the first dam on the Connecticut River. The draw here is the underground/under-river **viewing facility** that allows kids to watch salmon, shad, and other anadromous fish (those that migrate up rivers from

KELLY'S TOP FAMILY ADVENTURES IN THE PIONEER VALLEY

1. Skinner State Park, Hadley
2. Historic Deerfield
3. Riverside Park, Agawam
4. Basketball Hall of Fame, Springfield
5. Dino Land, South Hadley

the sea to breed in fresh water) pass by a window on their way to their favorite spawning grounds upstream. The facility (413–659–3714) is on First Street, on the south side of the dam, just before you go over the bridge; look for the sign. Open mid-May through mid-June, Wednesday through Sunday. Just below the dam, **Unity Park** is a nice spot for a picnic; there's a playground here, too.

Famous Bill's (30 Federal Street/Route 5, Greenfield; 413–773–8331) serves down-home food—meat loaf, burgers, and such—in a friendly atmosphere, with very reasonable prices and a kids' menu. Open for lunch and dinner daily, 11:00 A.M.–11:00 P.M.

DEERFIELD

Deerfield has survived more than just 300 years of farming in New England's unpredictable climate. In 1675 the Bloody Brook Massacre battle of King Philip's War resulted in 67 Deerfield residents' deaths. In 1704, just after the village had begun to recover from this catastrophe, a band of French and Indian soldiers attacked, killing 49 of the inhabitants and carrying off 111 more to Quebec. Miraculously, a few of these people survived and were able to make their way back to Deerfield. As a result of these early devastations, Deerfield's residents have long memories and a tight grasp on their families and possessions. Fortunately for us, they also realize that their knack for historic preservation is a valuable gift that's worth sharing.

Twelve of the restored eighteenth and nineteenth-century houses along The Street form an association called **Historic Deerfield** (Route 5/ The Street, Deerfield; 413–774–5581), which is open to the public year-round. These spectacular examples of eighteenth- and nineteenth-century architecture, design, furnishings, and lifestyles will probably be most interesting to older kids (especially those who have worked on home-renovation projects) who can appreciate the work that has gone into these houses, as well as the rich history of the town and its inhabitants. Don't try to see more than three houses in one day; they're all worth visiting, but more than three would be too much for any but the most ardent historic preservationist, let alone a family with children. Admission (good for two consecutive days) is $10.00 for adults and $5.00 for kids ages six to twelve.

Wolfie's (205 South Main Street, South Deerfield; 413–665–7068) has great sandwiches and a calm atmosphere. Open for lunch and dinner year-round, Monday through Saturday, 11:00 A.M.–10:00 P.M.

The **Yankee Candle Company** (Route 5, South Deerfield; 413–665–2929) began in 1969 in a kitchen here, and the rest is history—at least, the company thinks so. At this complex that seems to sprout new buildings every season, you can dip your own candles, visit a car museum and a Bavarian Christmas village, take a ride on a double-decker bus, and, of course, buy candles. For an idea of what a money-making operation this complex is, look at the large building at the left of the entrance to the parking area—it's marked EMPLOYEE FITNESS CENTER. Open year-round, daily, 9:30 A.M.–6:00 P.M.

MASSACHUSETTS'S CROSS-COUNTRY SKIING MECCA

Some of the state's best cross-country skiing is in the Pioneer Valley region.

Northfield Mountain Cross-Country Ski Area (Route 63, Northfield; 413–659–3713) has 26 miles of trails. Rentals are available.

Swift River Inn (151 South Street, Cummington; 413–634–5751 or 800–632–8038) has good snowmaking on much of its 10 miles of

Kids can learn the centuries-old art of bobbin lace making at the Hall Tavern at Historic Deerfield. (Photo by Amanda Merullo/Courtesy Historic Deerfield)

trails. This is one of the state's best-known touring centers; trails are well established. The ice skating rink is illuminated for night skating. *Note:* This is also a nice place to hike, bike, and fish during the summer.

Stump Sprouts Ski Touring Center (West Hill Road, West Hawley; 413–339–4265) has 12 miles of well-groomed trails on 450 acres of beautiful property. Instruction and rentals are available here. The lodge provides snacks and rentals; lessons and guided tours are also available.

The **Worthington Inn** (Old North Road/Route 143, Worthington; 413–238–4441) is a three-bedroom B & B that's strategically located near an excellent cross-country ski center (more below). The building was restored by the same person who directed the restoration efforts in Old Deerfield.

Hickory Hill Ski Touring Center (Buffington Hill Road, Worthington; 413–623–5535) consists of a 500-acre farm with about 12 miles of carefully groomed trails and a funky old lodge. During snow season it's open Friday through Monday.

Skinner State Park (Route 47, Hadley; 413–586–0350). A road—and several hiking trails—leads to the summit of Mt. Holyoke, where there's a great picnic spot with tables, a few grills, and a superb view of the Connecticut River Valley. **Summit House** (413–253–2883; open weekends May through October) is a recently restored old mountain inn that's now the site of summer concerts; from Route 47 follow the signs for Summit House. The park is open May through October, Monday through Friday, 8:00 A.M.–dusk, and weekends, 10:00 A.M.–dusk.

NORTHAMPTON, AMHERST, AND SOUTH HADLEY

Families with near-college-age children will find lots to do here, especially if the kids are interested in visiting any of the "five colleges"—the University of Massachusetts (which everyone calls UMass), Amherst College, Hampshire College, Smith College, and Mt. Holyoke College. Campus tours are given several times a week, if not daily, at most of the colleges.

When you arrive in Northampton, take a walk though the lovely campus of **Smith College** (off Elm Street). Art lovers will enjoy a visit to the fine **Smith College Museum of Art** (Elm Street; 413–584–2700), whose fine collection of more than 18,000 works of art are displayed

KELLY'S TOP ANNUAL EVENTS IN THE PIONEER VALLEY

1704 Weekend at the Indian House, February, Deerfield; (413) 774–7476

Basketball Hall of Fame Enshrinement Weekend, May, Springfield; (413) 781–6500

Salmon and shad spawning migrations, June, Turners Falls; (413) 659–3714

Up-Country Hot-Air Balloon Fair, July, Greenfield Community College, Greenfield; (413) 773–5463

Turn-of-the Century Ice Cream Social, July, Deerfield; (413) 774–7476

Teddy Bear Rally, August, Amherst Town Common; (413) 256–8933

The Big E (Eastern States Exhibition), September, West Springfield; (413) 737–2443

Kielbasa Festival, September, Fairfield Mall, Chicopee; (413) 594–2101

Greenfield Fall Festival and Street Fair, October, Greenfield; (413) 774–2791

Book & Plow Festival, October, Amherst; (413) 253–0700

Chrysanthemum Show, second week of November, Smith College, Northampton; (413) 585–2740

Bright Nights, December, Forest Park, Springfield; (413) 733–2251

in an outstanding building. Mid-September through May, it's open Tuesday through Sunday, 10:00 A.M.–5:00 P.M.; June, open by appointment only; July and August, open Tuesday through Saturday, 10:00 A.M.–5:00 P.M. Free.

If you have a poetry fan in the family, be sure to walk by the **Emily Dickinson Homestead** (280 Main Street, Amherst; 413–542–8161), on the campus of Amherst College. Dickinson was born and spent most of her life in this house, quite literally. Afternoon tours are given on Wednesday and Saturday afternoons, but you must reserve your spot ahead of time. Alternatively, visit the **Jones Library** (43 Amity Street, Amherst; 413–256–4090). The library's Special Collections rooms hold a precious store of handwritten works by Dickinson, as well as a comprehensive collection of papers and other articles owned by Robert Frost, another native of Amherst. Open Monday through Friday, 11:00 A.M.–1:00 P.M. and 2:00–5:00 P.M. Free.

Here's an unusual museum—in an old brownstone on Main Street, the **Words and Pictures Museum** (140 Main Street, Northampton; 413–586–8545) displays outstanding examples of "sequential art," which most of us would call comic strips. Aspiring artists and writers will be inspired by the highly creative works. Open year-round, Tuesday through Sunday, noon–5:00 P.M. Admission is $3.00 for adults and $1.00 for kids under eighteen; on Tuesday and Wednesday it's $1.00 for adults and free for kids.

Just across the street is **Ben and Bill's Chocolate Emporium** (141 Main Street, Northampton; 413–584–5695), where you can indulge in handmade chocolate treats that are made right on the premises.

Beyond Words Bookstore (189 Main Street, Northampton; 413–586–6304) has an excellent children's section.

True to its name, the **Soup Kitchen Café** (159 Main Street, Northampton; 413–584–4458) always has at least three homemade soups listed on the blackboard—sandwiches, salads, and some hot entrees, too. There are a few wooden tables in back, but much of their business is to go. Open Monday through Saturday, 11:00 A.M.–7:00 P.M., and Sunday, noon–5:00 P.M.

Look Memorial Park, on Route 9 in Florence (just northwest of Northampton), is a 150-acre conservation area with many water activities available—swimming, canoeing, and paddleboats—as well as a miniature railroad, an outdoor theater where summer concerts are held on most weekends, a small zoo, and lots of picnic tables and grills. Open dawn to dusk. Parking costs $1.00 on weekdays and $2.00 on weekends.

South Hadley is home to **Mt. Holyoke College,** the nation's oldest college for women. The campus is beautiful and well worth touring. Stop at the **Arboretum** (open daily, free) to see the greenhouse and the latest blooms.

To visit **Dino Land** (off Route 116, South Hadley; 413–467–9566), follow the directions on the enormous painted sign on the east side of Route 116. Carlton Nash grew up hearing his father talk about the dinosaur tracks that he'd seen on his family's property as a child. One day Nash decided to see if there was any truth to his father's stories. He followed the tracks to a nearby quarry, where he found even more. Fascinated, he bought the quarry and began to dig up the fossilized tracks of dinosaurs as small as a rabbit foot and as large as, well, what we think of when we think of a dinosaur's foot. As it turns out, the sediment and climate in this area of the Connecticut River Valley acted as a perfect preservative material for the tracks left behind by the dinosaurs who fed in the area millions of years ago. Kids love this place.

Berkshire Bed and Breakfast (413–774–3329) is a reservation service that inspects all host homes regularly to be sure that they meet their stringent standards of cleanliness and hospitality. Accommodations range from working farms to modest suburban dwellings to gracious Victorian homes.

HOLYOKE

Mt. Tom State Reservation (off Route 5, Holyoke; 413–527–4805), follow the signs from Route 5. The views are spectacular from the summit of Mount Tom, which your family can reach via a 3½-mile round-trip hike, a walk that you will probably share with lots of other families. Alternatively, the hike to Goat Peak is shorter (2 miles round-trip), less crowded, and easier for small kids. There is a small natural history museum near the trailhead and, at the peak, a watch tower that naturalists use to observe hawk migrations and that your family can use to look for birds or simply to enjoy the panoramic views of Mt. Tom, the river valley, and, on a clear day, the mountains of southern New Hampshire and western Massachusetts.

Also at Mt. Tom is a fifteen-trail, six-lift **ski area** (Route 5, Holyoke; 413–536–0516) that offers day and night skiing, and a ski school (413–536 –1575). The vertical drop is not very high, so trails here sometimes seem wider than they are long. This makes Mt. Tom a good place for beginners and intermediate skiers. During the summer there are tube rides, a water slide, and a wave pool. From Memorial Day through June, open weekends, 10:00 A.M.–8:00 P.M.; in July and August, open daily, 10:00 A.M.–8:00 P.M.

Like Lowell, Holyoke is a mill city, planned around the canals built in the early nineteenth century as the power source for the Holyoke Water Power Company. The 150-year-old system is still in operation, providing power to the city and supplying process water to manufacturing companies that occupy the old mill buildings. **Holyoke Heritage State Park** (221 Appleton Street, Holyoke; 413–534–1723) is an eight-acre complex of enormous mill buildings and outdoor spaces, with exhibits about the city's growth. There are two main attractions for families here. The first is the antique **Holyoke Merry-Go-Round** (413–538 –9838), in 1929 in Philadelphia. Housed in a colorful new building near the entrance to the park, the large carousel has forty-eight horses and two chariots, all carved by hand, plus a loud, cheerful band organ. Open year-round. The fee is $1.00 per ride.

Farther into the complex, the **Children's Museum** (444 Dwight Street, Holyoke; 413–536–KIDS) emphasizes family participation in educational games and interactive exhibits. Make your own paper or try your hand at one of the mock-ups of local businesses set up here, including a "working" TV station. Open Tuesday through Saturday, 10:00 A.M.–4:30 P.M., and Sunday, noon–5:00 P.M. Admission is $3.50 per person.

Volleyball was invented in Holyoke. In 1995 the game's centennial was celebrated at the **Volleyball Hall of Fame** (221 Appleton Street, Holyoke, 413–536–0926), in the Children's Museum complex, where displays include a look at current international competition; a historical exhibit about the game's founder, William Morgan; and a chronological examination of the game's development into an Olympic sport. Open year-round, Tuesday through Friday, 10:00 A.M.–5:00 P.M., and Saturday and Sunday, noon–5:00 P.M.

SPRINGFIELD

Another sport was born in the Pioneer Valley in the 1890s. Dr. James Naismith invented basketball when he made a game of throwing a soccer ball into a peach basket at Springfield College in 1891. The **Naismith**

Outdoor festivals throughout the year make for great times in the Pioneer Valley.
(Courtesy Greater Springfield Convention and Visitors Bureau)

Basketball Hall of Fame (1150 West Columbus Avenue, Springfield; 413 –781–6500) memorializes that fact in an entertainment center/museum that will be interesting to any visitor who's ever had even a remote connection to the game. Walk through the Shoe Tunnel, which is hung with the enormous footwear of inductees. Challenge your basketball knowledge. Shoot hoops of various shapes, sizes, and heights. Play Bill Walton in the Virtual Reality game. Or compare your height and arm span to those of the game's biggest players. The Hall of Fame is open daily, September through June, 9:00 A.M.–5:00 P.M., and July through Labor Day, 9:00 A.M.–6:00 P.M.; closed major holidays. Admission is $8.00 for adults, $5.00 for kids seven to fifteen, and free for kids under seven. Directions: Take exit 4 off the Massachusetts Turnpike to Route 91 South, take exit 7, and then follow the signs.

In Springfield's Quadrangle, a complex that incorporates four museums and the main branch of the Springfield City Library, the **Springfield Science Museum** (22 State Street, corner of State and Spring streets, Springfield; 413–739–3871) is a neat place to spend a few hours on a rainy day. The African Hall is full of examples of the diverse wildlife of the African continent. Dinosaur Hall will probably be the kids' favorite part of their visit to the Quadrangle, however, for here the full-size replica of a tyrannosaur towers over everyone. Other attractions of the museum include a hands-on Exploration Center, a planetarium, an antique airplane, and several interactive life science exhibits. Parking is free at the museums' and library's lots on State Street and Edwards Street. Open year-round, Wednesday through Sunday, noon–4:00 P.M. Admission (includes entry to all four museums) is $4.00 for adults, $1.00 for kids six through eighteen, and free for kids under six.

Montori and Company (5 Dwight Street, Springfield; 413–733–4511) is a good lunch spot that's not far from the museum complex. Homemade soups and a relaxed environment can be found here.

Also in Springfield is **Forest Park** (Route 83, off Route 21/Sumner Street; 413–733–2251), a large city park with a small zoo, nature trails, lots of picnic spots, swimming pools, and other recreational activities. During the December holidays the park has several drive-through **lighting displays** with various themes, such as the North Pole and Barney's Victorian Village. Cost is $6.00 per car.

SOUTH OF SPRINGFIELD

Riverside Park (Route 159/Main Street, Agawam; 413–786–9300 or 800–370–7488) is an enormous (more than forty rides on 170 acres) amusement park, New England's largest. It can be terribly crowded on summer weekends, but the tumult can add to the experience if you're prepared with comfortable clothes, sunblock, and a stroller for the little ones. There are four water rides, three roller coasters, a monorail, a Ferris wheel, two Kiddieland areas, a nice old merry-go-round, and a speedway (auto racing) on the grounds. Also here are lots of daily performances of the magic show, singalong, and puppet variety. No pets, no picnicking. Open weekends only from April 3 through Memorial Day and from Labor Day through October, 11:00 A.M.–11:00 P.M.; open daily, from Memorial Day through Labor Day, 11:00 A.M.–11:00 P.M. Admission (includes all rides) is as follows: Everyone more than 54 inches tall, $19.99; shorter than that but older than three, $10.99; three and under, free.

The Berkshires

Covering the western end of Massachusetts, Berkshire County changes dramatically, from the high mountains and isolated valleys in the north to the hilly forests and farmland of the area along the Connecticut border. Tell the kids to keep an eye out for the carved wooden Indians that "guard" the tourist shops along the Mohawk Trail, the steep scenic road cutting through the mountains between Greenfield and Williamstown. Willamstown, known for Williams College and its world-class art museums, is a classic New England village of white churches and clapboard houses along the edges of the town green. To the southeast is Mt. Greylock, the state's highest mountain, part of a huge park full of hiking trails of varying difficulties, as well as waterfalls, fishing areas, and campgrounds.

The southern Berkshire area is gentler in topography and more cultural in nature. The region abounds with museums, theaters, and outdoor classical music venues, the most famous of which is Tanglewood, summer home of the Boston Symphony Orchestra. Kids will marvel at the round stone barn at Hancock Shaker Village outside Pittsfield. Farther south, in Stockbridge, take the time to walk along the long porch and through the enormous lobby area of the rambling old Red Lion Inn.

During the winter Berkshire County is a mecca for skiing families. Three of New England's best small-scale, family-oriented downhill ski areas are here: Brodie Mountain, Butternut Basin, and Jiminy Peak. All can boast

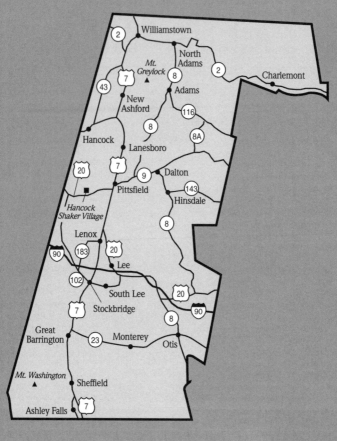

Williamstown

② 2

Mt.
Greylock ▲

North
Adams

⑧ 8

② 2

Charlemont

43

⑦ 7

New
Ashford

Adams

116

⑧ 8

8A

Hancock

Lanesboro

20

⑦ 7

⑨ 9

Dalton

Pittsfield

143

Hinsdale

Hancock
Shaker Village

⑧ 8

Lenox

90

183

20

Lee

102

South Lee

20

90

⑦ 7

Stockbridge

⑧ 8

Great
Barrington

23

Monterey

Otis

Mt. Washington ▲

Sheffield

Ashley Falls

⑦ 7

The Berkshires

of excellent ski schools, family packages, and reasonably priced accommodations either at the base of the mountain or within a few miles.

MOHAWK TRAIL

The Mohawk Trail, Route 2, is the highway version of the path that Native Americans used to travel from the Connecticut River Valley to the Hudson River Valley. Sixty-seven miles long, the road is only partially in the Berkshires, since it begins in the Connecticut River Valley. The trail is much more dramatic when you drive it from east to west.

As the road begins climbing into the foothills, look back over the Connecticut River Valley. If you want a wider-ranging view, stop at the tall white wooden **Longview Tower,** with observation decks that provide views of three states. Ask the kids which states these are (answer: Massachusetts, Vermont, and New York).

Kids love to ski in the Berkshires. (Photo by Rosenthal)

In the riverside village of Shelburne Falls, a quick detour off Route 2, see the **Bridge of Flowers.** It's a 400-foot retired trolley bridge that has been planted with flower beds. Perhaps the kids can think of other unused transportation facilities that could be rejuvenated in this way!

Right on Route 2, **Gould's Sugar House** (Route 2, Shelburne; 413–625–6170) is a good breakfast- or lunch-break stop along the Mohawk Trail, especially if pancakes and syrup sound good to you. Open daily March through October (except May), 8:00 A.M.–2:00 P.M.

Back on Route 2, the **Mohawk Trail State Forest Visitors Center** (Route 2, Charlemont; 413–339–5504) has lots of information and a good picnic area.

Zoar Outdoor (Charlemont, 800–532–7483), an experienced and enthusiastic whitewater-tour company, offers a variety of trips, from true whitewater adventures to calmer river trips on the Deerfield, West, and Millers rivers. They make and pack the lunches, give you instruction and equipment, and help every member of the party have a great day on the water. Afterward take a shower back at their base camp. There's a campground on the property for whitewater diehards who want to spend more than just one day on the water. Call ahead.

Turn north on Route 8A in Charlemont to see the 160-foot-long **Bissell Bridge,** one of the few remaining covered bridges in the Berkshires.

Just beyond Charlemont on Route 2 is a 900-pound bronze statue of an Indian chief figure with his arms and face lifted to the east. The piece is called **Hail to the Sunrise.** He's one of many Indian-chief statues that you'll see along the Mohawk Trail.

After Charlemont the trail passes by the entrance to the **Hoosuc Tunnel,** which was the longest railway tunnel in the country when it was completed in 1875. An engineering marvel in its time, the Hoosuc Tunnel was the first construction to use nitroglycerin. The highest point on the trail is the **Whitcomb Summit,** at 2,240 feet. If the kids are into ascending another observation tower (this one is much smaller than the one in Greenfield), it's 50¢ per person. In **Florida** stop at the Eastern Summit Gift Shop—not for the shop, but for the telescope (25 cents for about three minutes) on the edge of the steep hill that overlooks the northern Berkshires.

The trail makes several hairpin turns on its way into **North Adams.** The City of Spires, as residents like to call it, is a bit run down nowadays; the beautiful old brick factories and warehouses are mostly empty. Several of these buildings will soon be the home of the **Massachusetts Museum of Contemporary Art,** which everyone already calls Mass MoCA (the entrance is at 87 Marshall Street; 413–664–4481).

If your family includes a railroad buff or two, visit the **Western Gateway Heritage State Park** (Route 8, North Adams; 413–663–6312). Along with interesting tidbits about North Adams's history as a bustling railroad town, you'll learn about the construction of the aforementioned Hoosuc Tunnel. Open daily, year-round (except the last two weeks of January), 10:00 A.M.–5:00 P.M. Free.

On the grounds of Western Gateway Heritage State Park is the **Freight Yard Restaurant** (413–663–6544), serving burgers, pasta, and a local favorite, kielbasa. You can eat outdoors during warm weather. Open year-round.

Be sure to visit **Natural Bridge State Park** (off Route 8, North Adams; 413–663–6392). Sixty feet above a rapid stream in a deep, narrow chasm is a 30-foot-long, 15-foot-thick white marble natural bridge that was formed and smoothed by a glacier 500 million years ago. It's fun to walk down to the water via a series of bridges. July through August, it's open daily, 10:00 A.M.–6:00 P.M.; late May through June, and September through mid-October, open daily, 8:00 A.M.–4:30 P.M. Parking costs $2.00 per car; picnicking facilities are available in the park.

Twin Sisters Inn (1111 South Street/Route 8, North Adams; 413–663–6933) is a nice old country house that features four large guest rooms, two sharing a bath. Kids are welcome to romp on the ten acres of property that surround the house. Open year-round; please call ahead. Rates are $50–$60.

At **Miss Adams Diner** (53 Park Street, North Adams; 413–743–5300), you can have breakfast (best: waffles) or lunch (bests: fish-and-chips and meat loaf) in an authentic 1943 lunch car. Open year-round, Tuesday through Saturday, 6:00 A.M.–3:00 P.M., and Sunday, 7:00 A.M.–1:00 P.M.

From North Adams you can choose to continue west on Route 2 to Williamstown, or you can turn south on Route 8 toward Pittsfield.

WILLIAMSTOWN

Williamstown is about as different from its neighbor, North Adams, as two New England towns can possibly be. Whereas North Adams is a somewhat dilapidated version of its former bustling self, Williamstown hasn't changed much since the late nineteenth century. It's home to one of New England's best small liberal arts colleges, Williams College, and to two exceptional art museums.

The **Sterling and Francine Clark Art Institute** (225 South Street, Williamstown; 413–458–9545) has a world-class collection of late nineteenth-century paintings by Renoir, Monet, Corot, Pissaro, and Degas, among others. Also interesting is a room with paintings by the American artists Sargent, Remington, and Homer. They were contemporaries, and all were celebrated in their time for very different styles and subject matter: Sargent for his exquisite portraits of high-society figures; Remington for his depiction of cowboys and western life; and Homer for his haunting New England sea and mountain scenes. Open year-round, Tuesday through Sunday, 10:00 A.M.–5:00 P.M. Free. In July and August a gallery talk takes place every day at 3:00 P.M. The beautiful grounds are a great spot for a picnic.

Speaking of picnics, the **Store at Five Corners** (corner of Routes 7 and 43, Williamstown; 413–458–3176) has great sandwiches and dessert goodies, all packed to go. Open year-round, 8:00 A.M.–7:00 P.M.

The **Williams College Museum of Art** (Main Street, Williamstown; 413–597–2429) is one of the best college art museums in the country, in terms of the breadth of its collection of contemporary and modern American and non-Western art. The museum's ARTWORKS program, a series of one-person exhibitions of contemporary art, has been particularly well received. Good traveling exhibitions stop here, too. Open Tuesday through Saturday, 10:00 A.M.–5:00 P.M.; Sunday, 1:00–5:00 p.m; and major holidays that fall on Monday. Free.

At the **Williamstown Theatre Festival** (mailing address, Box 517, Williamstown 01267; box office, 413–597–3400), from late June through August, one of the country's preeminent theater groups presents musicals, dramas, children's theatre, and special events, often performed by nationally known actors. Most performances are at Williams College's Adams Memorial Theater, but call ahead to check.

KELLY'S TOP FAMILY ADVENTURES IN THE BERKSHIRES

1. Hancock Shaker Village, Pittsfield
2. Mt. Greylock State Reservation, Lanesborough
3. Mohawk Trail
4. Sterling and Francine Clark Art Institute, Williamstown
5. Tanglewood Music Festival, Lenox

Within walking distance of the Williams College campus and the museums, the **House on Main Street** (1120 Main Street, Williamstown; 413–458–3031) welcomes families. It's a six-room B & B: Three rooms have private bath; the other three share one full and one half bath. A hearty breakfast is served in the kitchen. The big screened-in porch is a nice spot to relax in the early evening. Rates run $75–$90.

Hobson's (15 Water Street, Williamstown; 413–458–9101) has a barnlike feel to it (in terms of its decor, not its clientele!) and a good variety of food on the menu, from chicken prepared in various ways to homemade soups to an abundant salad bar. Kids can order a half-plate of anything. Open Tuesday through Sunday for lunch and dinner.

MT. GREYLOCK

Mt. Greylock State Reservation (visitor center is at Rockwell Road, Lanesborough; 413–499–4262 or 499–4263) is an enormous park (10,327 acres), with 45 miles of hiking trails of varying difficulties, as well as camping, fishing, canoeing, cross-country skiing, and snowmobiling.

There are several ways to approach the mountain; one is from North Adams (1 mile west of North Adams on Route 2, take Notch Road through a residential area that turns into woody hills; signs will direct you from there); the other is via Route 7 in Lanesborough (follow the signs to the visitor center). The visitor center in Lanesborough is an excellent first stop. A large tabletop relief map shows the park's layout and topography, and an extensive selection of maps, many of them free, are available. The park is open from sunrise until a half-hour before sunset. The visitor center is open daily, 9:00 A.M.-5:00 P.M. from mid-May through mid-October, and 8:00 A.M.– 4:00 P.M. on weekends and holidays from mid-October to mid-May.

Even if your family hasn't done a lot of hiking, don't be discouraged by the mountain's height and breadth. Many of the park's trails leave from the parking area on top of the mountain (this is one of the reasons it's such a terrific family place; you can drive right to the best part). One of the best routes is a 4-mile hike from the summit down Overlook Trail to Hopper Trail and then on to March Cataract Falls. Coming back up, you can walk part of the Appalachian Trail rather than retracing your steps along the Hopper Trail. *Note:* The weather can change quickly and unexpectedly on Mt. Greylock. Every year a few experienced hikers find themselves stranded. Get a map and talk to rangers in the visitor center before you begin your hike.

Whether or not you hike, don't end your visit to Mt. Greylock without climbing the **War Memorial Tower.** On a clear day you'll be able to see Mt. Monadnock in New Hampshire, 115 miles away, as well as the full Berkshire range, the Taconics in New York, and the southern part of the Appalachians. The access road closes in mid-November (or earlier if snow demands it). The tower is open 9:00 A.M.–5:00 P.M. daily, from mid-May through mid-October.

From May through October as many as thirty-two people can sleep overnight at Greylock's **Bascom Lodge** (413–743–1591 or 443–0011). The lodge, built in the 1930s, sits atop Mt. Greylock, which, at 3,491 feet, is the highest point in the state. The eight rooms are rustic but comfortable, and they vary in size from dormitory-style rooms that sleep eight people to private doubles. All rooms share baths. Breakfast, lunch, and dinner are available at the lodge. The lodge is managed by the Appalachian Mountain Club, whose staff offer guided nature walks and hikes from here. Call ahead. Open mid-May through mid-October. Rates are $70–$80 per room.

CENTRAL BERKSHIRES

Savoy Mountain State Forest (260 Central Shaft Road, Florida; 413–663
–8469) is a smaller, less crowded version of Mt. Greylock State Reservation.
The park is especially appealing to children because of the good swimming
in North Pond (there isn't much legal swimming on Greylock). Hiking is
less challenging, too, and there are three cabins on the banks of South Pond.
The pleasant hike to **Tannery Falls** brings you to one of the nicest falls in
the Berkshires. Follow the signs from Route 116 in Savoy. Open year-round.

Brodie Mountain (Route 7, New Ashford; 413–443–4752; conditions, 413–443–4751) is known for its lively Irish approach to everything.
It's especially fun to ski here on St. Paddy's Day, when the snow magically
turns green and people named Kelly ski free. There's a ski school and day-
care program (hourly, half-day, or full day). Vertical drop is 1,250 feet.
There are twenty-eight trails, nearly all beginner and intermediate; the
black diamonds aren't tough. Six lifts. Night skiing, too.

Nice condominiums and an inn with 105 suite-type rooms are slope-
side at **Jiminy Peak** (Corey Road, Hancock; 413–738–5500 or 800–882–
8859; conditions, 413–738–PEAK), a self-contained resort that's so well
run, it seems bigger than it is (Jiminy counts a conference facility among its
amenities). The skiing is more challenging than at Brodie: The intermediate
runs are steeper, and black-diamond slopes deserve their rating. There's a
kids-only area where kids from four to twelve take their first SKIwee lessons.
You can enroll kids between six and fifteen in an eight-weekend program
that provides instruction with the same teacher. A snowboard park and an
ice skating rink are here, too. The day-care center takes kids from six months.
The state's first quad chair is here, along with one triple chair, three doubles,
and a J-bar. Vertical drop is 1,140 feet. There is night skiing throughout the
season. During the summer the **Alpine Slide** is a fun alternative to skiing.

Crane Paper Company (Housatonic Street, off Route 8, Dalton;
413–684–2600) makes the paper on which all U.S. currency is printed.
Tour the museum to learn how paper is made and see a display about the
history of paper money. Open June through mid-October, Monday through
Friday, 2:00–5:00 P.M. Free.

Dalton House (955 Main Street, Dalton; 413–684–3854) is a del-
uxe inn that's perfect for families who want luxury with their ski vacation.

There are eleven rooms (all with private bath, some with fireplace) in two buildings. The rooms in the carriage house are larger and quieter, with period furniture and exposed beams. During the winter, ski packages that include dinner are available. Winter and spring rates are $58–$85; summer and fall, $68–$115.

A few miles southeast of Dalton on Route 8 is the small town of **Hinsdale,** whose claim to fame is **Israel Bissell.** Bissell is the man who outdid Paul Revere: In five days he rode from Hinsdale through Connecticut to New York and on to Philadelphia to carry the news of the colonists' confrontation with the British in 1775. Bissell is buried in the Maple Street Cemetery (take Route 143 West; the cemetery is at the top of the first small hill after Route 8).

From June through early September, the **Pittsfield Mets,** a Class A farm team of the New York Mets, play at Wahconah Park (105 Wahconah Street, Pittsfield; 413–499–6387) three or four times a week. This is old-time baseball in a park that's so small, every seat is a good seat, and where the players are happy to sign autographs. Games are usually at 7:00 P.M. For a schedule, write to Box 328, Pittsfield 01202.

Our culture reveres the Shakers for their simple, beautiful furniture and building designs. What most people don't know is that their crafting skill was a direct expression of their religious devotion. Every chair they made, every load of laundry they washed, and every field they plowed was made, washed, and plowed as well as possible to express their reverence by making their environment a "heaven on earth." **Hancock Shaker Village** (junction of Routes 20 and 41, Pittsfield; 413–443–0188) was the third of eighteen Shaker communities established in the United States. Its heyday was in 1830, just after the round stone barn was completed, when 300 Shakers lived, worked, and worshiped here. They farmed, sold seeds and herbs, manufactured medicines, and made and sold all types of goods, from boxes to textiles. Eventually their population dwindled, and in 1960 the Shaker ministry in Canterbury, New Hampshire, sold the Hancock property to a group of Pittsfield residents who are dedicated to preserving the contributions of the Shakers to American life. The following year they opened Hancock Shaker Village as a museum.

You can tour twenty restored buildings on the property. It's best to join a tour; the austere settings are so beautiful that it's hard to understand the underlying ingenuity of Shaker design unless it's pointed out to you. During the children's tours (ages five to twelve; summer only) and workshops, kids learn how the Shakers spun wool, made clothespins, and washed 300 sets of clothes every day. The staff is knowledgeable, dedicated, and enthusiastic; tour guides have been known to convince the most tone-deaf visitors to try to sing "Simple Gifts" with the rest of the group. Open daily from April 1 through November 30, 9:30 A.M.–5:00 P.M. Other seasons, call ahead; schedule varies with weather. A cafe is open during the season and occasionally during the winter. Admission is $10.00 for adults and $5.00 for kids six to twelve; family rate is $25.00.

SOUTHERN BERKSHIRES

The southern Berkshires have been a haven for the wealthy for well over a century, and the cultural life in the towns of Lenox and Stockbridge reflects their passions: music and theater. During the high season of July and August, kids can see more live performances here than they could in many large cities—and much of it goes on outdoors. There are several excellent museums; gracious historic inns for families with well-behaved children; and parks, wildlife sanctuaries, and good skiing.

Rockwell, chronicler of a well-scrubbed version of American life's ups and downs during the first half of this century, lived in Stockbridge for the last twenty-five years of his life. **Norman Rockwell Museum** (Route 183, Stockbridge; 413–298–4100) holds the largest collection of original Rockwells. The grounds are a pleasant spot for a walk or a picnic, whether you go into the museum or not. Outdoor sculptures are by Rockwell's son Peter. May through October, it's open daily, 10:00 A.M.–5:00 P.M.; November through April, open weekdays, 11:00 A.M.–4:00 P.M., and weekends, 10:00 A.M.–5:00 P.M. The studio building is open from May through October. Admission is $7.50 for adults, $2.00 for kids six to eighteen, and free for kids under six.

The restored 1902 Lenox railway station is the site of the **Railway Museum** and the **Berkshire Scenic Railway** (Willow Creek Road, Lenox; 413–637–2210), which has a few small exhibits and two large working model railways. The Berkshire Scenic Railway operates vintage railroad cars on part of the Housatonic Valley Line, which used to be the northernmost part of the New Haven Railway. Open weekends and holidays from June through late October, 10:00 A.M.–4:00 P.M. Train rides are on the hour. Museum admission is free; the train ride is $1.50 for adults and $1.00 for kids.

Across from the town green in Stockbridge is the **village cemetery,** where, among other local notables, the Sedgewick family is buried. In 1781 Thomas Sedgewick, a lawyer, successfully defended Elizabeth "Mumbet" Freeman, who became the first slave freed by law in the United States. The trial also rendered slavery illegal in Massachusetts. Mumbet is buried with the Sedgewick family in the "Sedgewick Pie," the family grave plot, so called because family members are buried in a circle with their feet in the center. Why? They hoped that when they sit up on Judgment Day, they will see each other before they see anything else.

Tanglewood Music Festival (West Street, Lenox; box office, 413–637–5165; info out of season, 617–266–1492). Tanglewood is the summer home of the Boston Symphony Orchestra, whose members, on summer weekends, perform concerts from the afternoon into the evening, often with the assistance of internationally known musicians and conductors. Most people who come to hear them sit outside on the lawn, arriving early with elaborate picnics and making a day of it. Some devotees choose to sit "inside," which means under the roof of one of the two buildings: the Shed (which is anything but), with seating for more than 5,000, and Seiji Ozawa Hall, with seating for 1,180. If your kids are lucky enough to have music-lovers for parents, your entire family will enjoy an outing to Tanglewood, especially on a warm summer evening when the BSO plays *The 1812 Overture,* complete with fireworks under the stars. Shed and Hall tickets range from $12–$70. Lawn tickets (purchased on site only) are $12–$16, depending on the event; lawn tickets for kids under twelve are free (four per family). Children under five are not allowed in the Shed or the Hall during concerts. Write ahead for a full summer schedule: Symphony Hall, 301 Massachusetts Avenue, Boston 02115.

Even if you don't stay at the **Red Lion Inn** (Main Street, Stockbridge; 413–298–5545), do take the time to walk along the porch and peek into

KELLY'S TOP ANNUAL EVENTS IN THE BERKSHIRES

Butternut Basin Kids' Festival, January, Great Barrington;
(413) 528–2000

Winter Week at Hancock Shaker Village, February, Pittsfield;
(413) 443–0188

Brodie Mountain Pro Cup Race, March, New Ashford;
(413) 443–4752

Shearing Days at Hancock Shaker Village, May, Pittsfield;
(413) 443–0188

Berkshire Theatre Festival, June through August, Stockbridge;
(413) 298–5536

Jacob's Pillow Dance Festival, June through August, George
Carter Road, Becket; (413) 243–0745

Tanglewood Music Festival, June through August, Lenox;
(413) 637–5165 or (617) 266–1492

Williamstown Theatre Festival, June through August,
Williamstown; (413) 597–3400

Your Hometown America Parade, July 4, Pittsfield;
(413) 499–3861

Sheffield Antiques Fair, second weekend in August, Sheffield;
(413) 443–9186

Tub Parade, September, Lenox

Autumn Farm Weekend, August, Pittsfield; (413) 443–0188

Mt. Greylock Ramble, first weekend of October, North Adams;
(413) 743–1881

the lobby. If your kids are well behaved and old enough to appreciate a neat old inn, treat yourselves to a stay at this quintessential rambling New England inn that many others try to emulate. Rooms vary in size from quite small to almost palatial; most have original Norman Rockwell paintings. Families will be happiest in the suite arrangements that have a connecting bathroom. The annex buildings tend to be quieter than the main inn building. Meals are served in the main dining room, in a smaller tavern-type dining room, and downstairs in a pub called the **Lion's Den** (live music here at night). Open year-round (very crowded in July and August). Rates are $70–$120.

The breakfast and lunch counter in **Shanahan's Market** (Elm Street, Stockbridge; 413–298–3634), an old-fashioned general store across the street from the post office, just off Main Street, serves plain food, nothing special—eggs, bacon, pancakes, sub sandwiches, and lots of local gossip if you listen carefully. Breakfast and lunch only.

At **Sophia's** (junction of Routes 7 and 20, Lenox; 413–499–1101) diners sit in booths to eat Greek-style pizza, salads, pasta, and well-stuffed sandwiches. Open Tuesday through Sunday, year-round.

The **Village Snack Shop** (35 Housatonic Street, Lenox; 413–637–2564) is a low-key breakfast and lunch place with homemade soup and good lunch specials.

There's not much that's Shaker-ish about **Shaker Mill Tavern** (Route 102, West Stockbridge; 413–232–8565), but the food is very good, the prices are reasonable, and the staff is prepared for kids. Open year-round for dinner.

Joe's Diner (63 Center Street, Lee; 413–243–9756) is open from noon to midnight daily, year-round, serving classic diner food—for example, open-faced sandwiches, fries and gravy, and ice cream sodas—in a traditional diner setting, all for low prices.

Historic Merrell Inn (1565 Pleasant Street, South Lee; 413–243–1794 or 800–243–1794), is not appropriate for young children, but families with teenagers who appreciate New England history will enjoy a stay here. The building was a private residence from 1794 until 1817, when it was converted into an inn. Between 1817 and 1857 the inn served as a stop on the Red Bird Stagecoach Line, which traveled from Winchester, Connecticut, to Stockbridge twice a week. South Lee was the next-to-last stop. The innkeeper keeps the guestbook from that period open to the current date; it's fun to see who was visiting the inn on this day 150 years ago.

The inn was completely restored in the 1980s, and it has won many historical preservation awards. The wide-plank floors are original, as are the fireplaces in several of the guest rooms and common areas. Carefully selected antiques are scattered throughout the inn—in guest rooms as well as common areas—but the effect is not precious. The inn feels comfortable and lived in rather than delicate or expensive. The wooden bird-cage-style bar in the breakfast room is the only surviving one of its kind. Breakfasts are delicious and filling. Open year-round. Rates in summer and fall, $75–$135; winter and spring, $55–$95.

Berkshire Botanical Garden (junction of Routes 102 and 183, Stockbridge; 413–298–3926) offers fifteen acres of gardens that vary from herbs to lilies to vegetables of all kinds. This is a different kind of green space that young children will enjoy: It's accessible to them because the plants are just their size. Picnicking is encouraged here. Open daily from May through October. Admission is $5.00 for adults and free for kids under twelve.

Pleasant Valley Wildlife Sanctuary (472 West Mountain Road, Lenox; 413–637–0320) has 7 miles of easy walking trails that wind through meadows and forests, leading to a series of ponds where beaver dams are clearly visible. Open year-round, Tuesday through Sunday, dawn to dusk. Admission is $3.00 for adults and $2.00 for children.

Crossed by the Appalachian Trail, **Beartown State Forest** (Blue Hill Road, Monterey; 413–528–0904) has good hiking, but its highlight is **Benedict Pond,** one of the region's best swimmin' holes. Open year-round. Parking is $2.00.

Monterey Chèvre (New Marlboro Road, off Route 23, Monterey; 413–528–2138) is a goat farm that sells a wonderful cheese, chèvre, from the shop on the premises as well as to restaurants and shops in the area. The kids will enjoy seeing the tiny baby goats, but parents should keep children well back from the fence to avoid nipped fingers.

Race Brook Lodge (864 Under Mountain Road/Route 41, Sheffield; 413–229–2916) is a restored barn with a variety of rooms (all with private bath) and suites, which are perfect for families. Take a walk from the lodge to the Race Brook Waterfall, then up to the Appalachian Trail. Rates are $79–$129.

Mt. Washington State Forest and **Bash Bish Falls** (Route 344, Mt. Washington; 413–528–0330). The latter is a great name for a neat place. From Route 23 South, turn right at the signs for Mt. Everett–Bash Bish Falls. Follow the road west to the foot of the mountain, then follow the signs for Bash Bish Falls. Turn into the second parking area. From here you can hike 1 mile, then clamber, climb, or walk down a stone stairway to see the 60-foot waterfall that plunges into a churning pool. Unfortunately, you can't swim here—too dangerous—but the boulders that border the falls are still a cool spot to relax on a hot day. Open daily, dawn to dusk. Free.

Otis Ridge (Route 23 West, Otis; 413–269–4444) is a small ski area oriented to family business. The vertical drop is only 400 feet, and there are just ten runs. Come here if you want your kids to learn to ski in an intimate setting; that's what Otis Ridge is all about. Experienced skiers will be bored.

Martin's (49 Railroad Street, Great Barrington; 413–528–5455) serves breakfast all day, along with lunch specials. Try the omelet made with Monterey chèvre, or the strawberry-banana pancakes, or the lentil stew.

Four Brothers (Route 7, Great Barrington; 413–528–9684) is part of a chain of Greek pizza places that covers upstate New York and northwestern Connecticut as well as the Berkshire region, serving delicious pizza and eggplant dishes, among others. This one is housed in a newer building than most of the others. Open for lunch and dinner, year-round.

ASHLEY FALLS

This tiny town near the Connecticut border is the site of two interesting attractions: the oldest dwelling in Berkshire County, the Colonel John Ashley House, and Bartholomew's Cobble, a national natural landmark.

Bartholomew's Cobble (off Route 7A, Ashley Falls; 413–229–8600) is an unusual natural hilly rock garden, studded with limestone outcroppings (the cobbles) and featuring distinctive flora, such as forty species of ferns and many wild flowers. Bird-watching is excellent here, due to the abundant plant life. There are 6 miles of hiking trails (the easygoing Ledges Trail is particularly pleasant for families with younger kids), picnic facilities, and a small natural history museum. The museum and information center is open from mid-April through mid-October, Wednesday through Sunday and holidays, 9:00 A.M.– 5:00 P.M.

Bartholomew's Cobble is a great place for a family picnic and outdoor fun.
(Photo by S.J. Dechart)

Colonel John Ashley House (Cooper Hill Road, Ashley Falls; 413–229–8600). is named for one of the first citizens of what was then the town of Sheffield, which was purchased in 1722 from Native Americans for 460 pounds sterling, three barrels of cider, and thirty quarts of rum. Ashley, a surveyor and lawyer, built his house in 1735. In 1773 the Ashley house was the site of the signing of the Sheffield Declaration, now considered the first "declaration of independence" from Britain. Now maintained by the Trustees of Reservations, the house features a collection of colonial-era tools and tableware. The colonial-style herb gardens are particularly interesting. Learn how seventeenth-century Americans used herbs for cooking meals, healing the sick, and freshening their homes. Open Memorial Day weekend through mid-October, Wednesday through Sunday and Monday holidays, 1:00–5:00 P.M. Admission is $5.00 for adults and $2.50 for kids.

GENERAL INDEX

ACTIVITIES INDEX

OUTDOOR ACTIVITIES

PERFORMING ARTS

PICNIC SPOTS

ABOUT THE AUTHOR

Freelance writer Kelly Spencer began her travel-writing career in Boston in an undergraduate writing class with an essay about the year she spent as an exchange student in Scandinavia. Since then she has studied, traveled, and worked in several states and on other continents, always returning to Boston. She contributed to four books about Massachusetts and New England before she began this, her first solo book project. Together with her husband and their young daughter, she has visited nearly every art museum, gallery, and beach in the state while mastering the art of defensive driving in Massachusetts. She writes for several travel-oriented newspapers and edits publications for a small liberal arts college.